<ooL STUFF FoR KIDS To PERFORM

Monologues, duologues, triologues, fourologues...and improvs

words and photos by

Anna Waters-Massey

with additional works by

Cleo Massey and Madelaine Waters

First published by Zeus Publications 2010
http://www.zeus-publications.com
P.O. Box 2554
Burleigh M.D.C.
QLD 4220
Australia.

The National Library of Australia Cataloguing-in-Publication

Author: Waters-Massey, Anna.

Title: Cool stuff for kids to perform.

ISBN: 978-1-921574-78-8 (pbk.)

Subjects: Children's plays.
Recitations.

Dewey Number: A822.4

© Cover Design—Anna Waters-Massey 2010
Proudly printed in Australia

THANKS

Special thanks to my students whose personalities, anecdotes and improvisations inspired me to write these scripts. Also thanks to them for allowing me to use photos of them throughout the book.

A big thanks to my gorgeous children, Cleo and Joey, whose language and behaviour appear frequently on the following pages.

Also thanks to Cleo and my niece, Madelaine, for contributing some of their own work to this book.

I'd also like to extend my gratitude to the team at Zeus Publications, especially Gail for satisfying my Virgo perfectionism.

A Note from the Author

I teach 7 to 16-year-old children performing arts, which includes improvisation, characterisation, role-play and short film work. This book came about because I found it very hard to find resources for my classes. Most of the scripts available seemed to be for high school and secondary students, or, if aimed at primary students, they were long plays for the entire class to perform.

I wanted monologues and short scripts for two to four people, so each student could have a real go at learning lines and acting. I didn't want them to be overwhelmed with a long script that would take all term to learn and perform.

My scripts are all around two to four minutes in length; perfect for eisteddfods, festivals, show reels and audition pieces, and not too daunting for younger students.

The scripts are written in kids' language for kids to perform. At times the language is colloquial and I make no apologies for that. My own children have been a great example of the way kids really talk! I spend hours with children and teens (mine and my students) and wanted to write performance pieces that were relevant to them. My students have embraced these scripts enthusiastically as they can relate to the language and characters portrayed in them. The scripts have been performed at numerous concerts, festivals, competitions and eisteddfods, achieving great results. Many of the scripts have also been made into short films and used for actors' auditions and show reels.

Most of the characters in the scripts can be easily adapted to either male or female, depending on student requirements. In addition, the ages of characters are purely a guideline and not at all set in stone. Some scripts have proven very popular and I have included different versions for one, two, three or four people. Some characters have also popped up a few times in different scripts so I have grouped them together in a section called 'School Stuff for Kids to Perform'. These scripts can be performed separately or in conjunction with each other.

I have also included some photographs to motivate improvisations. The kids love creating their own dramas and these photos are great starting points for them, as well as excellent springboards for scriptwriting. You will also find some raps in this collection, which work well as whole class pieces.

I have had great success with these scripts and my students love performing them; I hope that you will also enjoy them.

Contents

1

Duos

Trios

Fouros

Raps

School stuff for kids to perform

Monos

Duos

Trios

Fouros

THE BUS STOP

Mother: Gradually gets more impatient as time passes.
Laura: Inquisitive 6 year old who can't keep still.
Teen: In his own world. He has an iPod plugged in with headphones and is singing along and nodding in time with the music.
Nancy: Old lady who thinks everyone is being rude to her.

There is only room for three people on the bench at the Bus stop. Laura, her mother and the teen are already seated when Nancy enters later.

Mother: Stop fidgeting Laura and just sit still.

Laura: I'm bored.

Mother: Well, the bus should be here soon, just be patient a little longer.

Laura: I'm hungry.

Mother: (*To the teenager.*) Do you catch this bus often? Does it usually run on time? (*Teen doesn't hear because he's listening to his iPod. Mother tries to get his attention.*) Excuse me.

Teen: (*Pulls earplugs out.*) Huh?

Mother: Do you catch this bus often? Does it usually run on time?

Laura: Can I listen to your iPod?

Teen: (*Teen ignores Laura and answers the mother.*) Sometimes. I catch it in to town most days but last week it didn't even come on Friday.

Mother: Oh how annoying. Did you complain?

Teen: Nuh! What's the use? I ended up hitching a lift.

Laura: What's on your iPod? (*Teen ignores her, puts earplugs back in, gets a lolly out of his pocket, and eats it.*) I want a lolly.

Mother: I don't have any Laura, I'll get you something when we get there.

Teen: (*Chewing lolly, teasing Laura.*) MMmmm.

Laura: But I'm hungry now! I need to go to the toilet…Mummy…I need to go to the toilet.

Mother: Laura, you'll have to wait.

Nancy: (*Enters, looks at the bench and pokes the teen with her walking stick.*) Excuse me!

Teen: Oi, what are you doing?

Nancy: I'd like to sit down young man.

Teen: (*Pulls one earplug out.*) So would I.

Nancy: Where's your respect? Let me sit down please!

Teen: I was here first. (*Ignores her and listens to iPod.*)

Nancy: Didn't your parents teach you any manners?

Laura: He's rude, Mummy. (*Mother gestures sshh to her.*) But he is!

Teen: Rude, am I? Mind your own business, squirt.

Nancy: Let me sit down young man!

Laura: Mummy, I need to pee...

Mother: The bus should be here any minute, just hang on.

Laura: I can't... Mummy!

Nancy: (*Pokes the teen again with her walking stick. The teen turns his back to her.*) In my day youngsters showed respect for their elders. (*She pulls earphones out of his ears.*) Are you listening to me?

Teen: Oi. Leave me alone. I could do you for assault, you know?!

Mother: (*Trying to diffuse the situation.*) Laura, get up and give the lady your seat.

Laura: But Mummy...

Mother: For goodness sake Laura, just get up.

Laura: But Mummy....

Mother: (*Pulls Laura up off the bench to reveal a wet puddle. She whispers to Laura.*) Laura!! What have you done?

Laura: (*Whispers back.*) I told you I had to go to the toilet!

Mother: (*Pulls Laura back onto the seat embarrassed and hisses at her.*) Stay there! (*To the old lady.*) Here, have my seat.

Nancy: Finally someone with manners. (*She sits.*) I don't know, children these days. No respect...

Laura: Mummy I'm wet...

Nancy: Wander the streets till all hours...

Laura: Mummy I want to get changed.

Nancy: Throw parties and destroy their parents' houses, drive fast cars like hoons...

Teen: (*Gets out another lolly, and eats it teasing Laura.*) Mmm...these are the best.

Laura: I want a lolly. Mummy....Mummy.

Nancy: They should all have a curfew, that's what's needed.

Laura: (*Speaking over Nancy.*) I'm hungry...

Mother: Would you just shut up!

Nancy: (*Thinks the mother is speaking to her. She stands up in outrage.*) Well, I never...how rude...and you a young mother... (*Mother tries to explain but Nancy keeps talking.*) I can see why children these days grow up to be so rude if you are any indication of the parents these days. I think I'd rather walk than sit here with such rude, ill-mannered people.

Laura: Mummy.

Mother: Just shoosh, would you!

Nancy: Well I never! (*She walks off muttering under her breath.*)

Mother: Oh Laura, now look what you've done.

Laura: But I'm hungry and I'm wet and I want a lolly!!! (*Teen eats another lolly and teases her.*)

Mother: (*To the teen.*) Do you think this bus will ever come?

Teen: (*Shrugs.*) Probably not, I might hitch.

Mother: Come on Laura, let's go home. I can't take any more of this. (*They get up and go.*)

Laura: Yay, can I have some chocolate when we get home? I want to do some painting…will you play dollies with me?…

Teen: (*Looks around, shrugs and ambles off with his thumb out to hitch a ride.*)

THE NAUGHTY SPOT

Monologue for a little boy or girl

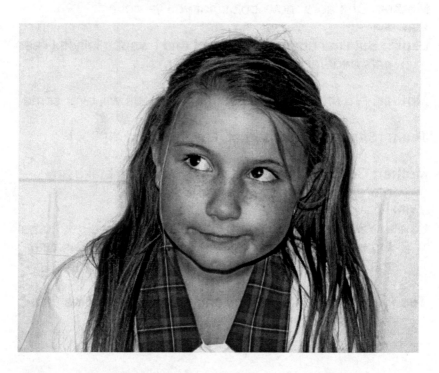

Deep breath. (*Inhales and exhales.*) Count to 10! 1, 2, 3, 4, 5, 6, 7, 8, 9, 10! (*Shouts out.*) Mum, can I come out now?

I hate the stupid Super Nanny. Ever since that dumb show came on telly Mum keeps sending me to 'The Naughty Spot'. So here I am...

It's not fair! She used to send me to my room which was much better 'cos I could play with my toys in there.

(*Shouts out.*) Mum, can I come out now?

Do you know why I'm in 'The Naughty Spot'?... Because I accidentally fed the dog some of my dinner...He was hungry! Gosh he only gets two meals a day! We get three as well as morning and afternoon tea. (*Shakes head.*)

The Super Nanny would say, "That behaviour is unacceptable, go to the Naughty Spot".

Television has a lot to answer for!

THE MAGIC NUMBER 8

Brie and **Nikki** are 12-year-old girls and best friends. Brie has a Magic Number 8 Ball, the kind you shake, ask a question and an answer is displayed on it.

Brie: Look what I got for my birthday! Can you believe it? (*She is holding a Magic Number 8 Ball and showing it to Nikki.*)

Nikki: OMG! Is it one of those Magic 8 Balls? I love them.

Brie: They are like fortune tellers. You can ask them anything and they will give you an answer.

Nikki: I know. Candice has one and she asked it if she would win the jellybean raffle at school, you know the one where you had to guess how many jellybeans were in the jar?

Brie: (*Brie nods.*) And…what happened?

Nikki: Well, it said she would, and guess what?

Brie: What?

Nikki: She did!

Brie: OMG!

Nikki: Also I heard that Miranda asked it if she would go to Fiji on holiday and it told her yes!

Brie: And she did, she left on Friday!

Nikki: I know! How do you think it works?

Brie: I don't know…it's just magic!

Nikki: Okay, you have to ask it something. Close your eyes, concentrate on your question and shake it.

Brie: (*Brie does what Nikki says then holds the 8 ball out to Nikki.*) What does that say?

Nikki: 'Without a doubt'…that means yes! What did you ask it?

Brie: Not telling…I'll shake it again and see what it says. (*She shakes it and looks again. Nikki peers over her shoulder.*)

Nikki: 'Most definitely!' That's yes again. What did you ask?

Brie: I can't tell.

Nikki: You asked if Brendan loves you, didn't you?

Brie: (*Nods.*) Don't tell anyone. I just have a feeling that he loves me because he keeps poking me and punching my arm.

Nikki: My mum says that means boys like you, it's just their weird way of showing it.

Brie: Really?

Nikki: Really!

Brie: Yesterday, he even grabbed my bag and threw it up a tree!

Nikki: OMG! He totally is in love with you!

Brie: Do you think so?

Nikki: YES!!

Brie: (*Holds the 8 ball up to Nikki.*) Here, you ask it something.

Nikki: Will I ask if Cody loves me? (*They both giggle, Brie nods.*) Does Cody love me? (*They giggle as she shakes the number 8.*)

Brie: 'It is decidedly so'. Huh?

Nikki: It means yes!

Brie: Do you like him?

Nikki: I don't know…he has nice eyes. (*They giggle.*)

Brie: Hey, let's ask it about Rosa. You know how she's always bragging, I'm sure she makes up things.

Nikki: Does Rosa really know The Veronicas? (*She shakes it.*) 'Very doubtful'…I knew she was making it up! She is such a fibber.

Brie: I know. She even told me that she went round to The Veronica's house for tea once!

Nikki: As if!!

Brie: Hey, I've got another one…does Jason B wet his bed? (*They are giggling as she shakes the 8 ball.*) 'Without a doubt!'

Nikki: (*Nikki shakes it.*) Will Brie and I be best friends forever?

Brie: What does it say?

Nikki: (*Reading.*) 'Very doubtful'.

Brie: Shake it again. But concentrate properly this time. Close your eyes…ask the question…now shake it.

Nikki: (*Reading.*) 'My reply is no'.

Brie: This is dumb, it's not working anymore.

Nikki: Yeah, that's weird 'cos it was right about everything else. Does it need its battery changing?

Brie: No, it doesn't have batteries.

Nikki: It's probably just getting worn out.

Brie: Yeah, Mum says toys don't last long these days...I know, let's give it a rest and then come back to it later.

Nikki: Good idea, it probably just needs a rest. (*They exit.*)

PLAYING SCHOOLS

Monologue for a young girl

Little girl has her dolls and teddies lined up in front of her as she marches in.

Now class, we have a very busy day today and you have to pay attention. Monique, are you talking?! (*She waits for an answer.*) Just as well. Now we will start with some maths. Who knows what two plus two equals?? Yes, anyone...James? (*She waits.*) Very good, four is the right answer.

Oh my goodness Jane, are you eating bubble gum? Put it in the bin right now.

Now Monique, stop poking Billy and tell me what three plus four equals? (*She waits.*) No, try again. (*She holds up her fingers, three on one hand, four on the other, then nods.*) Yes, very good. Try to concentrate in class.

Oh there's the bell. Off you go to morning tea, quickly now...Miss Cathy must rush to the staffroom or all the other teachers will get the scones and I will miss out! Quickly now... (*She claps her hands to shoo them away.*)

THOMAS BENSON

Thomas: 10-year-old schoolboy.
Miss Pembleton-Smith: Prim, strict schoolteacher in her late 40s.

Miss P-S is in the classroom and calls Thomas over to her desk.

Miss P-S: Thomas Benson, come here to me at once!

Thomas: (*Thomas ambles slowly up to Miss P-S.*) Yes, Miss Pembleton-Smith?

Miss P-S: For the past two weeks you have been consistently late for school, and today you arrived at lunchtime, with your uniform in a mess and no note of explanation from your parents. What is going on, Thomas?

Thomas: Well, Miss Pembleton-Smith, it's like this see…

Miss P-S: Yes!!!

Thomas: Well…

Miss P-S: Oh, get on with it boy!

Thomas: Well, me dad's been sick, right, and me mum has to leave for work at 6am and me dad likes to have Charlie in with 'im for company. (*Miss P-S winces at his bad grammar.*)

Miss P-S: And who the dickens is Charlie?

Thomas: Oh, Charlie's our dog Miss.

Miss P-S: What exactly has all this got to do with you being late?

Thomas: (*He draws it out trying to think up excuses.*) Welllll…every time I go to leave the house I have to get Dad to hold Charlie but as soon as I get to the corner Charlie comes running up to me. So I have to take 'im back to Dad.

Miss P-S: (*She snorts out loud in disbelief.*) Surely that does not make you three hours late for school!

Thomas: Well, Miss Pembleton-Smith, today was a bit different.

Miss P-S: Oh *do* get on with it Thomas, this is becoming very tedious.

Thomas: Today, Miss Pembleton-Smith, Charlie didn't catch up to me until I was on the school bus! Fair dinkum Miss! I was sitting up the back seat in my usual place when an old lady up the front of the bus screamed out (*acts out the old lady*), "Oh my, get it away from me. Aaagh…!!!" Charlie had jumped on the bus after me and was trying to climb on her lap to lick her face. (*He grins.*) He's so friendly.

Miss P-S: Yes, yes, get on with it Thomas.

Thomas: Well, I grabbed Charlie and the bus driver made me get off.

Miss P-S: I see that you had to take the mongrel home but that still does not excuse you for three hours. I am going to talk to the Principal... (*She starts to walk off.*)

Thomas: (*Thomas interrupts.*) But Miss Pembleton-Smith, I haven't finished telling you what happened next!

Miss P-S: I am running out of patience!

Thomas: As soon as we got off the bus, Charlie ran out on the road and there was a man on a motorbike coming the other way, he had to swerve to miss Charlie and when he did that he ran into a pole and fell off the bike. (*Miss P-S is shaking her head in disbelief.*) So I had to see if he was okay. That's how I got the oil and grease on me uniform.

Miss P-S: (*Correcting his grammar.*) *My* uniform! Really your grammar is appalling, Thomas!

Thomas: (*He shrugs and smiles.*) Well, as it turns out he was okay, the man on the bike, I mean, so I raced off to find Charlie. He had gone down to the park and jumped into the pond chasing a cat. Can you believe it, Miss Pembleton-Smith?

Miss P-S: I am having a great deal of trouble believing it, Thomas Benson!!!

Thomas: Well, I had to go in after him, that's why my shoes are all wet, Miss.

Miss P-S: (*Very sarcastically.*) Oh do go on, Thomas, I'm dying to hear what happened next!!

Thomas: (*Thinks he's on a roll now and continues excitedly.*) Well then I grabbed Charlie by the collar and hauled him outta the pond, then he goes and shakes himself all over me. That's why I'm all muddy and wet.

Miss P-S: Okay, alright so you took the silly mutt home and then came to school three hours late.

Thomas: Well not exactly…as it happens…

Miss P-S: (*Miss P-S interrupts him.*) I don't care, I don't want to hear another word. Since you are obviously so good at inventing stories I have an excellent idea for your detention. You must write for me a 500-word essay, with *correct grammar*, on your ridiculous mishaps, and have it on my desk by 9am Monday.

Thomas: But Miss…

Miss P-S: (*Holds up her hand for silence.*) Not another word. (*Imitating his poor grammar.*) Get *outta me* sight before I change *me* mind and send you to the Principal! (*Thomas runs out quickly.*)

EXCUSES, EXCUSES

Monologue for a boy or girl

I'm sorry I'm late, Miss Pembleton-Smith, it's like this, see. Well, me dad's been sick, right, and me mum has to leave for work at 6am and me dad likes to have Charlie in with 'im for company. Oh, Charlie's our dog, Miss. Welllll…every time I go to leave the house I have to get Dad to hold Charlie but as soon as I get to the corner Charlie comes running up to me. So I have to take 'im back to Dad. Well, Miss Pembleton-Smith, today was a bit different.

Today, Miss Pembleton-Smith, Charlie didn't catch up to me until I was on the school bus! Fair dinkum, Miss! I was sitting up the back seat in my usual place when an old lady up the front of the bus screamed out, "Oh my, get it away from me. Aaagh…!!!" Charlie had jumped on the bus after me and was trying to climb on her lap to lick her face. He's so friendly. Well, I grabbed Charlie and the bus driver made me get off.

But, Miss Pembleton-Smith, I haven't finished telling you what happened next! As soon as we got off the bus, Charlie ran out on the road and there was a man on a motorbike coming the other way, he had to swerve to miss Charlie and when he did that, he ran into a pole and fell off the bike. So I had to see if he was okay. That's how I got the oil and grease on me uniform.

Well, as it turns out he was okay, the man on the bike, I mean, so I raced off to find Charlie. He had gone down to the park and jumped into the pond chasing a cat. Can you believe it, Miss Pembleton-Smith? Well, I had to go in after 'im, that's why me shoes are all wet, Miss. Well, then I grabbed Charlie by the collar and hauled 'im outta the pond, and then he goes and shakes himself all over me. That's why I'm all muddy and wet. So Miss, I just thought I'd let you know what 'appened 'cos I 'ave to go 'ome now to get changed!!

PHONE TALK

Wendy: A typical browsing shopper.
Shopkeeper: 17–28 years old. Bored, pays no attention to her customers, would rather talk to her friends on the phone.

Wendy is wandering around the shop looking at things. The shopkeeper is on the phone.

Shopkeeper: (*Talking on the phone.*) Get out! No way! Did he know about it?…Oh Belinda is such a cow! She's so on herself anyway…I know…yeah like totally. (*Looks up at Wendy who is browsing, but says nothing.*) So like, he aksed her about this other guy and she like totally denied it???? Can you believe it?? (*Looks at Wendy.*) Are you right?

Wendy: Yep, just looking. Oh, actually do you have…? (*But she is too late as the shopkeeper is talking again on the phone.*)

Shopkeeper: No, it's alright, I'm listening…yeah, I've got a customer…No she's fine, just looking…

Wendy: Actually…um…excuse me… (*Tries to get shopkeeper's attention.*) Could I just ask you something?

Shopkeeper: (*To the phone.*) Hang on a minute…(*To Wendy.*) Yes?

Wendy: I was just wondering if you had any… (*Her phone rings and she searches her bag for it.*) Oh sorry, hang on a minute, I'll just get that. (*Shopkeeper rolls her eyes – how rude.*) Hi, Sharna, just hang on a minute, I'm in the cutest little shop…

Shopkeeper: (*On her phone.*) Oh, now she's on the phone…No, not Belinda…no, my customer. Yeah a bit rude, I was halfway through serving her!

Wendy: It's down on the highway, no, I guess I can talk for a minute…the shopkeeper won't get off the phone to serve me…so do you want to meet at the beauty salon at 4pm?

Shopkeeper: Yeah, we could go meet at the café after work, Belinda won't be there, will she?

Wendy: I'm not going if she's going to be there!

Shopkeeper: Let's get some of those nachos to share, and then we can have…

Wendy: A leg wax, my legs are getting so hairy now. Maybe I should get my eyebrows...

Shopkeeper: Dipped in chocolate. Yumm. That is soooo...

Wendy: Smelly? I know... it's the nail polish remover. I wish they could use something that wasn't so...

Shopkeeper: LOUD! I know! Last time I saw her, I like aksed her, "Belinda, could you just like talk a little softer, your voice is really hurting my..."

Wendy: Toenails... mmm...and maybe a manicure as well. Hello...hello...Sharna?...Oh damn, I've been cut off. (*Looks to the shopkeeper to get her attention.*) Um, excuse me...

Shopkeeper: Hang on a minute...

Wendy: Me?

Shopkeeper: No you, Wendy...(*Speaks into the phone.*)

Wendy: How do you know my name?

Shopkeeper: What? I don't know your name.

Wendy: Yes, you just called me Wendy.

Shopkeeper: Oh is your name Wendy?

Wendy: Yes, I just told you that.

Shopkeeper: Ha, that's hilarious!

Wendy: Well I don't like it much either, but I didn't think it was that funny.

Shopkeeper: (*Into the phone, laughing.*) The customer's name is Wendy!

Wendy: It's really not that funny.

Shopkeeper: (*To Wendy.*) No, you don't get it! I'm talking to Wendy.

Wendy: Yes I know and I'm talking to you...what's to get? It's not rocket science! (*Her phone rings again, she answers it.*) Hi Sharna, yeah we got cut off...

Shopkeeper: (*To the phone.*) I'm trying to explain to her that your name is Wendy and she doesn't get it...started talking about rocket science or somethink?! I know...what are the odds of that?...Hilarious...

Wendy: (*Whispering into her phone.*) This shopkeeper is so rude, she keeps laughing at my name...

Shopkeeper: So tell me more about Belinda...oh, how dare she?

Wendy: Do you think I should complain?

Shopkeeper: I shouldn't have to put up with that, should I?

Wendy: I shouldn't have to put up with that, should I?

Shopkeeper: Well, what do you think would happen if I said something?

Wendy: Well, what do you think would happen if I said something?

Wendy & Shopkeeper: (*They both look at each other and say into their phones.*) Hang on a minute…(*To each other.*) Would you stop doing that?!

Shopkeeper: (*Into the phone.*) Wendy, just shut up a minute!

Wendy: (*To the shopkeeper.*) I beg your pardon?

Shopkeeper: What?

Wendy: How dare you tell me to shut up! (*Into her phone.*) Did you hear that?

Shopkeeper: Of course I heard that, I'm not deaf…and I didn't tell you to shut up!

Wendy: You did. You just said "Wendy shut up!"

Shopkeeper: (*Starts laughing.*) Oh you thought I was telling you to shut up! Oh that's funny.

Wendy: It's not funny, it's rude. (*To her phone.*) Can you hear this?

Shopkeeper: I already told you there's nothink wrong with my hearing! (*To the phone.*) Wendy, I'm going to have to get back to you. (*She hangs up.*)

Wendy: (*To her phone.*) Oh now she won't even talk to me. Unbelievable!! I'm leaving. (*She walks out of the shop, still on the phone, muttering.*)

Shopkeeper: What on earth was her problem?

TALKING THE TALK

Sophie: 13 years old, she thinks she is the coolest and most worldly of the three girls.
Tammy: 12 years old, likes to act the fool.
Tayla: 12 years old, a bit unsure of herself.

The three girls are in Sophie's bedroom, lying on the floor and the bed chatting. At various times throughout the scene they paint their nails, brush their hair, try out hair clips, hold clothes up to themselves and look in the mirror.

Sophie: Did you guys see that awesome new boy?? Wow, is he wicked or what??

Tammy: Dur Sophie! You can't be serious, he looked like a freak to me.

Tayla: No way!

Tammy: Yes way!! Didn't you check out his glasses? He's a total freak!

Sophie: Helllooo girlfriend!! Tammy you are sooo uncool. His glasses were wicked. Everyone is like getting them now.

Tammy: Whatever!

Tayla: I was thinking of asking him to the school dance. What do you reckon?

Tammy: Eeeeoooooo gross! (*She pretends to gag.*)

Sophie: (*Ignoring Tammy.*) Go for it Tayla, he's sooo cute.

Tayla: Really?

Sophie: Totally!!

Tammy: Here, I'll pretend to be him. (*She picks up some sunglasses and puts them on.*) What's his name?

Sophie & Tayla: (*Say his name together giggling at Tammy.*) Jordan.

Tammy: Okay, I'll be Jordan and you like ask me to the dance, Tayla. (*She puts her hands in her pockets and strikes a cool pose.*)

Tayla: (*Approaches Tammy nervously.*) Hi, I'm Tayla.

Tammy: (*Using a boy's voice.*) G'day, I'm Jordan, how's it going??

Tayla: Fine!!

Tammy: Fine!

Tayla: Fine!!

Tammy: Fine!!!

Sophie: (*She interrupts*) A duh Tayla!

Tayla: Are you going to the dance next week?

Tammy: Dunno. Is it cool?

Tayla: (*Trying to be hip.*) Way cool, yeah it's rad. Do you wanna come with me?

Tammy: (*Playing up to her.*) Ooooh yeah baby...NOT!!!

Tayla: (*Picks up a pillow and hits Tammy, laughing.*) You dag!!

Sophie: What are we going to wear to the dance? I'm so not organised.

Tayla & Tammy: Same!

Tayla: Maybe I could borrow my sister's leather skirt.

Tammy: Nice! That skirt is sooo awesome.

Sophie: I'm like the same size shoe as Mum now, and check this out, she said I could wear her black boots.

Tammy & Tayla: Wicked!

Sophie: I want to do my hair like Britney Spears in that new film clip.

Tammy: That is such a cool do, I wish my hair was longer. I was thinking of like spraying it green to match my eyes and like tying it up like this. (*She fiddles with her hair.*) What do you reckon? (*The other two girls look horrified, then realise she is joking.*)

Tammy, Sophie & Tayla: (*They shout out together.*) NOT!!!! (*They all laugh.*)

Sophie: (*Getting up and putting on some lip gloss.*) Hey, do you want to go hang at the mall? We could get some Maccas (McDonalds) and just chill.

Tayla: Yeah, cool.

Tammy: Mmmmm Maccas.

Sophie: Okay girls…lips on. (*They all apply lip gloss.*) Sunnies? (*They all get their sunglasses out.*) Awesome…let's do it!!

Tammy: Maybe Jordan will be there, Tayla, and you can pop the question. (*She laughs.*)

Tayla: Not!

Tammy: Wicked! (*They walk off.*)

FOUR EYES AND TRAIN TRACKS

Amy: 11 years old, confident and funny.
Dylan: 11 years old, quiet and a bit shy.

Amy sees Dylan sitting all alone in the playground and comes over to him.

Amy: Hi chum, why so glum? (*Laughing.*) God, I'm so funny, I just crack myself up sometimes.

Dylan: Yeah. (*Keeps his head down.*)

Amy: So what's up? Why the big long face?

Dylan: You wouldn't understand. (*Turns away from her.*)

35

Amy: Try me.

Dylan: It's a waste of time.

Amy: (*Throws herself on her knees wailing.*) Oh nooo, he thinks I'm a waste of time. Woe is me.

Dylan: (*Smiles with his hand up to his mouth.*) Get up, you dag, everyone's looking.

Amy: Ha ha, I got you to smile. Now tell me what the problem is.

Dylan: (*Turns to her and does a big fake grin. She realises he has braces on his teeth.*) These are the problem.

Amy: (*Loudly, in mock horror.*) Oh my God, he has train tracks on his teeth! He's subhuman! Everyone run!!

Dylan: Shut up, everyone will hear!

Amy: So, they're just braces. What are you going to do, never talk anymore, keep your mouth closed, refuse all food, die a martyr for the cause???

Dylan: I knew you wouldn't understand.

Amy: What's to understand? So you have mouth jewellery? Cool! I bet they'll be off in six months.

Dylan: Twelve actually!

Amy: Well that's not so bad. Look what I have to wear for the rest of my life. (*She turns and puts on a pair of glasses.*)

Dylan: I never knew you wore glasses!

Amy: I haven't worn them yet, I got them last week and haven't had the guts to wear them.

Dylan: But they are cool. Harry Potter wears glasses and everyone likes him.

Amy: A dur Dylan, I'm kind of a girl, if you hadn't noticed!

Dylan: Yeah, but what I mean is, even girls think Harry Potter is cool. What about Nicole Kidman? I've seen her in glasses at a press conference. And that Charlies Angels girl, she wore glasses.

Amy: I suppose…

Dylan: Let's do a deal. I'll start smiling, talking and eating again if you wear your glasses.

Amy: Well… (*Thinking about it.*)

Dylan: And if anyone teases or hassles us, we stick up for each other.

Amy: Okay…deal, but you still have to stick up for me when you get your braces off!

Dylan: Deal. And when you're old enough you can get contact lenses or have laser surgery.

Amy: I don't know, now that I think about it I rather like the idea of looking more intelligent. Maybe my grades will improve.

Dylan: (*Looks at Amy doubtfully.*) I wouldn't count on it!

Amy: Shut up 'Train Tracks'!

Dylan: Just watch it 'Four Eyes'! (*They go off together laughing.*)

DARTH VADER IS COOL

Monologue for a young boy

(*Wearing Darth Vader mask and mimicking his voice.*) Aha…Luke Skywalker, I've been waiting for you. (*Pulls out*

sword.) Har! Your feeble skills are no match for the Dark Side. Prepare to be destroyed! (*Heavy breathing.*)
(*Lifts off his mask.*) It's only me really. Did I scare you? Darth Vader is so cool. I love Star Wars. Mum says she wishes I would play cowboys instead. What's a cowboy?? Is it a boy who is half a cow, like Mr Tumnus on The Lion the Witch and the Wardrobe?

Did you know Darth Vader turns out to be Luke Skywalker's dad?

(*Puts mask back on and mimics Darth Vader.*)
Luke, take off this mask so I can look on you with my own eyes. (*Takes mask off again and fakes dying dramatically.*)

TALES OF A PENCIL CASE

Pete the Pen: An engraved pen, which twists in the middle.
Georgia the Gel Pen: A shiny new gel pen with a lid and
silver sparkly ink. She has a Brother P Touch label
on her side with the owner's name on it.

Both pens roll onto the stage then engage in conversation.

Pete: Hi, my name's Pete the Pen, I haven't seen you
before.

Georgia: No, I'm new. My name's Georgia…the Gel Pen.
Beautiful colour, aren't I?

Pete: Silver sparkles are not really my thing. I prefer the
classic blue ink myself.

Georgia: Mmmm. (*Looks Pete up and down.*) Whatever. So
this is home is it, a Billabong pencil case? I suppose it
could be worse.

Pete: Too right it could. Yesterday I got picked up by
mistake by a grade 5 boy who put me behind his ear.

Georgia: Eeeeooo, was he sweaty?

Pete: Worse…he had nits! I've felt itchy ever since.

Georgia: How awful. I had a close call in the shop before I
was bought. There I was all shiny and new on the shelf
and a baby in a pram grabbed me…

Pete: Oh they really should keep us out of children's reach. The baby didn't put you…?

Georgia: Yep! Straight in the mouth! Slobbered all over me she did, and nearly swallowed my lid! Thankfully the mother retrieved it and put us both back on the shelf.

Pete: That was a close call. (*They both nod in agreement.*) Hey, what do you think of my engraving? (*He turns to show a name engraved on his side.*)

Georgia: Very nice, did it hurt?

Pete: No, not a bit.

Georgia: I just got this Brother P Touch label. (*She shows Pete.*) I'm not very happy with the colour, would have preferred a metallic look, this is so 90s, don't you think? Anyway, what's the goss in here…any romances I should know about?

Pete: Well, Mark the Marker Pen and Hilda Highlighter are an item. Been together since last term. Don't go near Sid the Stapler, he'll snap your lid off if he gets a chance.

Georgia: Oooh, nasty! Any erasers? I've always found them to be a fun bunch, all bouncy and happy.

Pete: Oh, Eddie's okay, but… (*He leans closer to Georgia.*) Edna has started seeing Reg the Ruler.

Georgia: No way, an eraser going out with a ruler!

Pete: Sssh, no one knows yet.

Georgia: (*Whispering.*) But it's not right, is it? I mean he's 30cm long. She would only be a fraction of that!

Pete: She says it doesn't matter, she's fallen for his straight lines.

Georgia: Well! (*They both appear to be thinking.*) Can I tell you something?

Pete: Sure.

Georgia: You mustn't tell anyone though.

Pete: Okay.

Georgia: In the shop, I had a fling with…a calculator!

Pete: (*Shocked.*) You didn't?!

Georgia: I did.

Pete: But they never mix with pens and pencils, not even felt pens or highlighters!

Georgia: (*Proudly.*) But I'm a gel pen. He loved my silver shimmer. He was so intelligent.

Pete: I'd never have a chance with a calculator, even with my beautiful twisty waist. (*He twists in the middle.*) Click tops are so common, don't you think? (*Georgia nods.*) The best I could hope for is a whiteout pen. They are so forgiving, you can never do wrong with one of them.

Georgia: So what's our owner like? She doesn't chew us, does she?

Pete: No, thank goodness, but you don't want to get lent to her best friend…she's a chewer. (*They both shudder.*)

Georgia: Woh…what's happening? (*They both fall to the ground and start rolling.*)

Pete: Must be lunch time. She's putting us away, watch out for the sharpener!

Georgia: Woh…here we go… (*They roll off stage.*)

Pete: Look out…paperclips on the move…

SORRY I'M LATE

Monologue for a boy or girl

I'm sorry I'm late, Mrs Henderson, but there's a really good reason. This morning we were all sitting down having breakfast as usual, when the most awful thing happened. Suddenly Dad keeled over in his chair. "Quick," Mum screamed, "ring the ambulance, he's having a heart attack!" So the next thing, I'm on the phone giving our address to triple zero.

The ambulance came zooming up the street with all the sirens going, very dramatic. Luckily, I was waiting outside waving frantically or they would have gone straight past. We all piled into the ambulance and took off for the hospital.

Then the worst thing happened! Mr Thomas' dog, Pluto, ran in front of the ambulance and we skidded to avoid him, narrowly missing old Mrs Turnbull with a shopping trolley, then finally we collided with a water pipe which then burst, squirting water over the entire street and ambulance.

Thankfully, poor old Dad was still out to it, with an oxygen mask strapped to his face and some sort of drug being pumped through an IV drip. Well, all of a sudden he started convulsing. Clearly, he was having some sort of reaction to the drug which was supposed to be saving his life. Then, as his arms and legs were flying all over the place, he kicked Mum in the nose, breaking it, and booted the ambulance man with such force that he flew out the back of the ambulance ending up in Mrs Turnbull's roses, with water

45

raining down on him from the burst pipe. Could things possibly get any worse!?

The police arrived just as Mum stumbled out of the ambulance with blood pouring out of her nose, then to our astonishment they grabbed the ambulance man who Dad had kicked out of the van, pulled the driver from the seat, handcuffed them and led them away. "Hey! What's going on?" I yelled. "My dad's in there having a heart attack and convulsions. You can't take them away."

"Oh yes we can," the cop replied. "They just robbed the Westpac Bank before picking you up!" Robbers, masquerading as ambulance men...what next?

Within seconds another cop car, a fire engine and another ambulance, thankfully manned by real medical staff, screeched into the street. The sirens were awesome! Anyway, everyone seemed to know what they were doing and we ended up in emergency at the local hospital. Dad's in intensive care in a stable condition, Mum's in casualty and has an ice pack on her nose and I'm clearly exhausted from the whole ordeal. Obviously you won't be able to contact either of my parents for quite some time but you can see why I'm late. Oh and I also forgot to bring in my assignment. Sorry...

FINE THEN, WHATEVER

Allison: A devious 8 year old.
Mum: Allison's mother, in her 30s.

The scene is set in Allison's home. Throughout the play Allison alternates between speaking directly to her mother and at other times to the audience.

Allison: I'm a kid, right, and I like things my own way so if I'm playing in my room and my mum says,

Mum: 'Allison, come and have tea now.'

Allison: I say, 'I'm playing in my room', and she says,

Mum: 'Well, dinner's ready, finish up and come to the table now!'

Allison: Well I figure it's time to chuck a tantrum, 'cos I don't want dinner now, I want to play. So here goes. 'I'm playing, I don't want dinner, leave me alone, you always spoil my fun!' Then Mum says,

Mum: 'If you don't come in here right now young lady, there will be big trouble when your father gets home. Now stop acting like a baby and get in here now!'

Allison: So I say, '**Fine then, whatever**!' And I go eat my dumb dinner. When I finish I want to go play again but Mum says,

Mum: 'Allison, where do you think you're going?'

Allison: 'To my room to play...'

Mum: 'Not until you've cleaned up your dinner plate, and have you done your homework yet?'

Allison: 'Mum!!! Can't I ever just play like a kid?'

Mum: 'Of course, just as soon as you do what I've told you to.'

Allison: So I figure another tantrum is due, 'Mum, you always pick on me, I don't ever get to play'. (*Throws herself on the ground and yells.*) 'Aaagghhh...' and she says in that scary voice,

Mum: 'All---is---on!!!'

Allison: So I say, **'Fine then, whatever!'** Finally when I've done all Mum's dumb jobs I get to play, and I'm having fun until...

Mum: 'Time to clean your teeth and hop into bed.'

Allison: 'Oh Mum, I don't want to, I want to watch the Simpsons.'

Mum: 'Bed time young lady, it's a school night.'

Allison: (*She looks at the audience with a sneaky grin.*) You guessed It... 'Aaagghhh, I don't want to go to bed, all the other kids at school get to stay up late.'

Mum: 'Your dad will be home any minute now, he's had a long day at work and he will...'

Allison: (*Cutting her mother off.*) **'Fine then, whatever!'** So I go clean my teeth and get in bed. Then Mum pokes her head round the door and says,

Mum: 'Now Allison, remember we have to go to the dentist in the morning before school to get that tooth seen to.'

Allison: 'No Mum, I don't want to, I hate the dentist, no.'

Mum: 'You have to go, the appointment is made and if you won't go, then I won't let you eat lollies ever again...' (*She pauses.*) 'Well??'

Allison: And then she says, as if she could read my mind, at exactly the same time as me,

Mum & Allison: 'FINE THEN, WHATEVER!!!'

FINE THEN, WHATEVER

Monologue for a young girl

I'm a kid, right, and I like things my own way so if I'm playing in my room and my mum says, 'Allison, come and have tea now.'

I say, 'I'm playing in my room.'

And she says, 'Well dinner's ready, finish up and come to the table now.'

Well I figure it's time to chuck a tantrum 'cos I don't want dinner now, I want to play, so here goes... 'I'm playing, I don't want dinner, leave me alone, you always spoil my fun!'

Then Mum says, 'If you don't come in here right now young lady, there will be big trouble when your father gets home. Now stop acting like a baby and get in here now!'

So I say, '**Fine then, whatever**!' and I go eat my dumb dinner.

When I finish I want to go play again but Mum says, 'Allison. where do you think you're going?'

'To my room to play.'

'Not until you've cleaned up your dinner plate, and have you done your homework yet?'

'Mum!!! Can't I ever just play like a kid?'

'Of course, just as soon as you do what I've told you to.'

So I figure another tantrum is due, 'Mum, you always pick on me, I don't ever get to play. Aaagh…'

Then she says in that scary voice, 'All---is---on!!!'

So I say, '**Fine then, whatever!**'

THE FREDDO CLUB

Shiloh: The one in charge of the group.
Angie: Shiloh's best friend.
Jacinta: A fun girl who is always up for a laugh.
Annie: The new girl to the group.
All the girls are approximately 12 years old.

Shiloh and Angie are sitting down cross legged with two
Freddo Frogs in front of them. Jacinta enters with Annie
tagging along after her.

Shiloh: You're late! We said 11 o'clock and it's 10 past!

Jacinta: Sorry. Mum made me empty the dishwasher.
(*Shiloh and Angie exchange glances and roll their
eyes.*) Anyway…this is Annie.

Annie: (*Waves shyly.*) Hi.

Jacinta: She wants to join the Freddo Club.

Angie: Did you both bring a Freddo?

Jacinta & Annie: Yes.

Shiloh: Put them in the middle then. (*They do as Shiloh
asks.*)

Angie: Okay, do you know the rules, Annie?

Annie: Jacinta told me a bit, but not really.

Shiloh: Alright…well, we're called the Freddo Club.

Jacinta: Duh, Shiloh, I think she knows that much!

Angie: Get to the fun part, Shiloh.

Shiloh: Well, we each have to tell a secret at each club meeting, and whoever tells the best one gets to have all the Freddos.

Jacinta: But we have one, big, important rule.

Angie: Whatever secrets we tell here, none of us are allowed to repeat to anyone else.

Annie: What if I find out a secret about one of my best friends though?

Shiloh: You can't tell them. Even if they are a good friend. That's the rules.

Jacinta: So...do you still want to join?

Annie: Yep.

Shiloh: Okay. Everyone...hands in. (*They all pile hands on top of each other in the centre of the circle*.) Now repeat after me, 'We at the Freddo Club solemnly agree, to keep our secrets indefinitely!'

All girls: 'We at the Freddo Club solemnly agree to keep our secrets indefinitely!' (*They remove their hands*.)

Shiloh: Alright, who wants to start?

Angie: I will. (*She pauses to make sure she has everyone's attention*.) I found out this week that two of our teachers are going out with each other!

Jacinta, Shiloh & Annie: WHO?

Annie: Mr Edwards and…(*She pauses, teasing them.*)

Jacinta: Miss Price? (*Angie shakes her head.*)

Shiloh: Not Mrs Cray?

Angie: She's married!!

Shiloh: (*Shiloh shrugs.*) Yeah, but she's always talking to him outside the library.

Annie: Who? Tell us!

Angie: Miss Grundy!!! (*The girls squeal with delight.*)

Jacinta: How do you know?

Angie: Well, my mum was talking to Toby's mum, who is really good friends with Miss Grundy's sister. And she said that Miss Grundy and Mr Edwards are in the same basketball team and last week they went out together afterwards for a drink!!

Annie: Wow! Maybe they'll get married.

Jacinta: Eeeeoooo, gross!

Annie: I think it's romantic. (*They are all giggling.*)

Jacinta: I won't be able to stop giggling when I see him in class tomorrow.

Shiloh: Jacinta, remember you can't say anything.

Jacinta: I know, but I can think it! (*She keeps giggling.*)

Angie: Alright, who's next?

Shiloh: Me. I'll go next. Guess who is leaving our school because they didn't get the lead role in the musical next term?!

Jacinta, Angie & Annie: Rebecca Holloway!

Shiloh: How did you guys know? I only found out this morning at ballet.

Angie: That's old news, Shiloh. I knew that on Thursday.

Annie: Yeah, me too.

Jacinta: Beat ya! I found out Wednesday at netball training!

Shiloh: Oh. (*She is disappointed.*) Well I guess I won't be winning the Freddos today...

Jacinta: Okay, my turn. Unless you want to go next, Annie?

Annie: No, it's okay, you go.

Jacinta: Okay then. I heard that Rachel Bennett's brother in grade 12 took his dad's new BMW last night without permission, went hooning up the highway with five friends in the car, skidded off the road, 'cos he was going so fast, then crashed into another car! And...guess who was driving the other car???...the Principal, Mr Harvey!

Shiloh: No!!

Jacinta: Yes!!

Annie: Oh my gosh!!!

Angie: That is so not true, Jacinta!

Jacinta: Is so! My brother told me this morning.

Angie: I stayed at Rachel's last night and that most
definitely did not happen!

Jacinta: (*Jacinta looks shocked.*) My brother told me!

Angie: Well he's lying! Rachel's brother and **one** friend went
to the video shop in the dad's new car, **with the dad**,
and then came straight back. There was no crash and
no mention of Mr Harvey, the Principal.

Jacinta: I'm gonna kill Robbie when I get home.

Shiloh: (*Laughing.*) He got you a beauty, Jacinta, you're so
gullible! (*The others laugh too, Jacinta is a bit
embarrassed.*) Okay Annie, looks like Angie's going to
win the Freddos unless you've got a better secret?

Annie: Well...

Angie: Come on Annie, don't be shy.

Annie: It's kind of personal...

Jacinta: We won't tell anyone. We promise. (*The others nod
in agreement.*)

Annie: Okay...well...last week...my mum and dad told me
that they don't love each other anymore and they're

going to get divorced. (*She looks like she will cry and the others are shocked into silence.*)

Jacinta: Oh Annie…

Shiloh: You poor thing.

Angie: Maybe they'll go to counselling and make up?

Annie: (*Shakes her head.*) They tried that already and it didn't work.

Jacinta: That totally sucks, Annie.

Annie: I know.

Shiloh: I'm sure everything will work out okay.

Angie: Yeah, they'll probably get over it. (*Shiloh and Angie look at each other awkwardly.*)

Shiloh: Anyway, your secret's safe with us.

Annie: Thanks. (*She looks embarrassed.*) I better go now 'cos my little brother has soccer.

Jacinta: I'll walk you home.

Shiloh: Here Annie…you take the Freddos.

Annie: Thanks. (*She takes them and goes out sadly.*)

Jacinta: I'll go and make sure she is okay. (*She follows Annie. Once they are a little distance from the others they burst out laughing and share out the Freddos.*)

Jacinta: You were so believable! That was hilarious.

Annie: I know, I almost believed myself. Do you think we should go back and tell them?

Jacinta: No not yet, wait till we finish the Freddos first! (*They exit laughing.*)

NOTHING TO DO

Cleo: 8-year-old girl.
Jessica: 8-year-old friend visiting Cleo for a play.
Katie: Another 8-year-old friend visiting Cleo.

The girls are in Cleo's bedroom surrounded by toys and games.

Cleo: What can we do? There's nothing to do!

Jessica: We could play with the PlayStation?

Katie: No, I'm so sick of that. What else can we do? (*Thinks for a minute.*) I know, we could play Bratz dolls.

Jessica: Nah...we already did that. Let's go outside.

Cleo: It's too hot.

Katie: Let's paddle in the canal then.

Cleo: No, it's all slimy. Why don't we climb that big tree out the front?

Jessica: I don't want to, I've got a skirt on. (*Pauses and thinks.*) There's nothing to do!

Katie: Let's go play on the scooter.

Jessica: That's not fair because I haven't got mine here.

Cleo: We could take it in turns?

Jessica: That's boring for me. What else can we do? (*Has an idea.*) Let's play hide and seek.

Cleo: It's too hot! I already said that.

Katie: Well what about we get some of your games down from the cupboard like 'Mousetrap' or 'Trouble'?

Cleo: Then I'll just have to put them all away again. Let's draw.

Jessica: But none of your felt pens work properly and the pencils were all blunt last time we drew pictures. I'm soooo bored!!

Katie: Me too. There's nothing to do!!

Jessica: What about we go play on the trampoline or swings?

Cleo: We'll just get all sweaty and even hotter. We could go under the sprinkler?

Jessica: I didn't bring my bathers.

Cleo: You can wear some of mine.

Jessica: They wouldn't fit me.

Katie: Let's play some CDs and make up a dance.

Jessica: Yeah, let's do that. What CDs do you have?

Cleo: They're all dumb, I'm so sick of them all, let's do something else. I know, let's play on the computer?

Jessica: I'm so sick of the computer!!! Anyway it's too hot in the computer room. Oh boy Cleo, there's nothing to do!!

Cleo: What time is it? Are there any kids' shows on TV yet?

Katie: No it's too early. (*Jessica shows Cleo her watch.*)

Cleo: Oh no Jessica, it's nearly 2 o'clock! Your mum will be here to pick you both up in a minute!!

Jessica: Oh no, now all our time is gone and we haven't even played anything!

COFFEE, PLEASE

Amelia and Kate: Two girls in their teens.
Waitress: Snooty, late 20s.

The two girls enter a rather posh café and are about to sit down.

Amelia: Oh this table's nice, let's sit here Kate.

Kate: Excellent! We can people watch from here. (*They are about to sit down when the waitress appears.*)

Waitress: Are you here for lunch, ladies?

Katie: No, just coffees thanks.

Waitress: Well you can't sit here, these tables are only for our dining patrons, you'll have to sit over here. (*She leads them to a table at the back, in a corner.*)

Amelia: Could we have a glass of water first please?

Waitress: We don't provide water, you need to buy it by the bottle.

Kate: How much is it?

Waitress: (*Rolls her eyes.*) $5.50, Madam.

Amelia: (*Looks at Kate in disbelief.*) We'll skip that then, let's just get coffee, Kate.

Kate: Yeah, I'm dying for one.

Waitress: What type of coffee would you prefer?

Amelia: Just two white coffees thanks. (*Kate nods in agreement.*)

Waitress: (*Very sarcastically.*) Will that be two lattes, two flat whites, two cappuccinos, mocaccinos, viennas, macchiatos, affoggatos, mellachinos, frappes, iced, brewed or percolated?

Kate: Cappuccino for me.

Amelia: Yeah same.

Waitress: Now would you prefer full cream milk, skim milk, soy milk, rice milk, skinny milk or goat's milk?

Amelia: (*Both girls look a little confused.*) Just normal milk, do you have that?

Kate: Yeah, I'll have normal milk too.

Waitress: (*Scribbles on her pad.*) Now are we wanting decaf, caffeinated, double decaf, strong, weak or...

Kate & Amelia: (*Look at each other puzzled then at the waitress.*) Ummm...

Waitress: (*Very sarcastically.*) **Normal** coffee I presume??

Kate & Amelia: (*Both nodding and starting to giggle a bit.*) Yes please.

Waitress: (*Sarcastically.*) I presume madams would like chocolate sprinkles on their cappuccinos? (*Both girls nod and try not to giggle.*) You'll find the sugars in the bowl here. (*She gestures to the centre of the table.*) There is an assortment of raw sugar, fine white sugar, sugar cubes, brown sugar, Equal and a range of artificial sweeteners. I'll be back with your order momentarily. (*Waitress leaves.*)

Kate: Oh my God!! (*She bursts out laughing and they mimic the waitress.*) Would madams like soy milk, goat's milk, pig's milk..?

Amelia: Dog's milk, horse's milk?

Amelia & Kate: (*Laughing hysterically they say together.*) Elephant's milk!!

Kate: I never knew ordering coffee could be so hard!

PIANO LESSONS

Monologue for a young boy

On Wednesday after school I have to do piano lessons and all I really want is to play rugby with all the other kids in my class.

(*He mimes playing with the right hand.*) C, D, E, F, G

G, F, E, D, C (*He mimics the teacher.*) 'Again boy, faster!'

C, D, E, F, G, G, F, E, D, C

My teacher is Mr Blackwell. He's old and cranky and has hair growing out of his nose and ears instead of on his head. Mum says, sometimes that happens when you get old. (*Mimicking his mother.*) 'He's a great pianist and has been playing since he was a little boy.'

If that's what happens when you play piano all your life I'd definitely rather switch to rugby!

CANNOT READ DISC!

Shopkeeper: Bored young man 18 to 20 years old.
Jed: Boy who just wants some good service.

The scene is set in a video rental shop. The shopkeeper is playing a game on his Nintendo and alternately checking his computer for msn messages from his mates. The boy enters the shop and stands at the counter waiting to be noticed.

Shopkeeper: (*Writing on the computer.*) Ha, yeah right as if! (*He keeps typing and doesn't notice Jed.*)

Jed: (*Coughs out loud.*) Cough, cough. (*Still gets no service.*) Cough, cough. (*He clears his throat.*) Ahemmmm.

Shopkeeper: (*Without looking up.*) Yeah, just stick it in the returns chute.

Jed: Um, but I want another one.

Shopkeeper: (*Still doesn't look up from computer.*) Yeah, just go pick one then.

Jed: But I want to return this one and get another one.

Shopkeeper: (*Finally looks up.*) Yeah! Like I said, stick it in the return chute, then go pick another one.

Jed: But I want to swap this one...

66

Shopkeeper: (*Cuts him off, and talks to him as if he's stupid.*) Soooo...stick it in the return chute, then go pick another one. (*He goes back to his computer.*)

Jed: Um...but I already took this one out this morning and my mates are coming round and we want to watch it this evening...

Shopkeeper: (*Cuts him off.*) Yeah well it's not due back till tomorrow so you don't have to return it yet.

Jed: What I'm trying to tell you is, it doesn't work!

Shopkeeper: What doesn't work?

Jed: This DVD.

Shopkeeper: Why doesn't it work?

Jed: I don't know. It just doesn't. It gave me a message...

Shopkeeper: (*Cuts him off again.*) Well it should work. I can't see why it doesn't. Did you have your DVD player turned on?

Jed: What? Yes, Of course I did. It had a mess...

Shopkeeper: (*Cuts him off again.*) So did you have your television on AV?

Jed: Yes! A message came up that said...

Shopkeeper: (*Cuts him off again.*) So you had a message then? Why didn't you say so?

Jed: I did, but you kept cutting me off. It said...

Shopkeeper: (*Cuts him off again.*) Well...what did it say? This message.

Jed: (*Getting cranky, he says quite forcefully.*) CANNOT READ DISC.

Shopkeeper: Woh! Okay matey. No need to yell at me.

Jed: I'm not yelling. Just trying to get you to understand me.

Shopkeeper: Alrighty then. Can I have a look at the disc? (*Jed hands it over and he puts it in the player behind the counter.*) Nup, this disc isn't working. Did you scratch it?

Jed: No! It never worked!

Shopkeeper: Oh, is that right, is it?

Jed: Yes!

Shopkeeper: Well how do I know that you didn't scratch it.

Jed: Because I'm telling you...

Shopkeeper: (*Cuts him off again.*) How do I know that you didn't watch it already with all your mates and then scratch it while you were being careless getting it out of the DVD player?

Jed: Are you serious?

Shopkeeper: Yep!

Jed: Look, can you just give me another disc without scratches on it?

68

Shopkeeper: Well I'm not really sure that I can do that.

Jed: Okay! Look! I came in here two hours ago and hired this poxy DVD that does not even work and I want a replacement one that is not faulty. Is that too much to ask!?

Shopkeeper: Oooh feisty, aren't we?

Jed: Or do I need to get my dad to come back with me? (*He looks at his name badge.*) Eddie, isn't it? I think you know my dad…Sergeant Bennett? I think you might have met him last week…at the drag racing at the Spit!!

Shopkeeper: Okay, okay, pushy little beggar aren't you.

Jed: The DVD?

Shopkeeper: Look I don't normally do this…

Jed: Fine, whatever…

Shopkeeper: I'm supposed to write up a report when returns are faulty…

Jed: (*Gets out his mobile phone and starts dialling.*) I'm gonna get my dad to sort this out…

Shopkeeper: But for you…here ya go. (*He hands him a replacement DVD.*) Why not keep it for the week, eh?

Jed: Thanks. Pleasure doing business with you. (*He walks out.*)

THE DENTIST

Monologue for a boy or girl

Ugghhh...just the smell of this place gives me the creeps. You'd think they could burn some incense or something to cover the smell of disinfectant. (*Sits down.*) And what's with the boring magazines? Readers Digest. Please! Haven't they heard of Disney comics? I mean, here we are at the dentist who specialises in children's teeth and the best they can do is leave out a few Readers Digests and put some crummy video on the TV about health insurance! Bo - or - ring!

Uh oh, did you hear that? The drill! Just the sound of it makes me feel sick. They should choose a nicer name for the drill. All I can think of is Dad's big Makita work drill when I hear that word. Let's face it, the sounds are even worse than the smell of this place.

Oh. Someone's coming out. Crikey, he doesn't look too good. Is that a tube of toothpaste he's holding? Oh get out!! Is that what the dentist gives you? What about lollies or a sticker, at least my doctor knows what kids like. This dentist needs a lesson in child friendly tactics.

Last time I went to the doctor's, I had chicken pox and he gave me a whole container of jelly beans. It was so cool! It even had a sticker on it where I could write my name so no one else could pinch them. Mum said it was a specimen jar and hoped it hadn't been used.

I think I'm up next...yep, that's my name. Okay, here goes (*stands up*)...oh no, all of a sudden I don't feel too good, I need to sit down...oh I must have caught a bug or something. Mum...I don't feel well, I think I'm going to be sick...no really, there's a bug going round the school...seriously Mum, I wouldn't make it up...here, feel my forehead, I have a fever...okay, okay I'm going but don't blame me if I throw up on the dentist!

SICK

Mum: Caring, but wise to what is going on.
Jack: 8 to 12 year old who really doesn't want to go to
school.

Jack is sitting at the breakfast table while his mother is
getting all the breakfast things ready.

Jack: (*Coughing.*) I really don't feel good, Mum.

Mum: Why, what's wrong?

Jack: (*Coughs again.*) I have an awful cough and my throat
hurts.

Mum: (*Comes over to him.*) Let me see, open your mouth,
now say ah… it looks alright to me.

Jack: But it really hurts. (*Starts to make his voice croaky
and coughs a few more times.*) Can't I stay home?

Mum: Jack, you only have a little cold. That doesn't mean
you need to stay home. (*Puts down cereal and a hot
Milo for Jack.*) Here's your cereal and a nice hot Milo.
That will make you feel better.

Jack: But I feel awful, my head is all dizzy and my nose is
blocked up.

Mum: (*Puts her hand on Jack's forehead.*) You feel alright to
me. Let me get the thermometer. (*She gets the
thermometer from the cupboard while Jack does a few
more fake coughs, then comes back and puts it in his*

mouth.) Now just hold it there for a moment under your tongue. (*As his mother turns to make herself a cup of tea, Jack gets the thermometer and puts it in his hot Milo. With the other hand he pinches his cheeks to make them redder. Quickly he puts the thermometer back in his mouth as his mum turns around.*)

Mum: Now let's see. (*She looks at the thermometer.*) Oh my goodness, it is high and your cheeks look a bit flushed too.

Jack: I told you I didn't feel good.

Mum: Wait a minute, why is the thermometer all sticky? (*She looks carefully at it.*) Is that Milo? Jack, did you put this in your Milo?

Jack: (*Looks at his mother with big, sick cow eyes and speaks in a croaky voice.*) I really feel bad, Mum.

Mum: You really are the limit, Jack. Fancy pretending you have a temperature!

Jack: Please, can't I stay home, I'll only get worse at school, I'll just sit on the couch in the lounge and watch videos, I won't bother you, please...

Mum: Alright. If you feel that bad you can stay home. (*Jack thinks he has won.*) But if you're really sick you have to stay in bed, in your room. That's what sick people do.

Jack: But Mum...I'll be bored.

Mum: Too bad, if you're sick you should be in bed.

Jack: But lying on the couch is the same as lying in bed!

Mum: No way, the deal is you can stay home if you stay in bed, otherwise eat up and get ready for the bus…Well??

Jack: (*Realising his mum has won.*) Alright. I'll go but don't blame me if I infect the whole school! (*He storms off leaving his mother looking amused.*)

LOST

Monologue for a young girl

Mum? Mummy? Mummy! Where are you? (*Louder.*) Mummmmm!

I can't find my mother. She was here a minute ago. (*Yells.*) Mummmm! (*Softer.*) Mummy.

We came to the shopping centre together to get my dad a birthday present. She was right beside me a minute ago. (*Calls out again.*) Mummm! She was just looking at the CDs and DVDs over there, and I just needed to look to see if the new Bratz doll was in here yet. You know the one. She is so

75

cool, her name is Jasmin but I think you say Yasmin like the J is a Y. She has this groovy velvet jacket with fur on it and all this gorgeous long hair. When I grow up I am going to change my name to Jasmin (*she pronounces it as Yasmin*) and I'm going to dye my hair just like hers.

Oh is that my mum over there? Nup, she's just got the same skirt on. (*Softly, to herself.*) Mummy, where are you?

I guess I should just stay here with the dolls and she'll find me. (*She looks around.*) But I've been here for ages....maybe something happened to her...maybe she tripped over and broke her leg...or a bad guy grabbed her and kidnapped her. She could have had an asthma attack and been taken off in an ambulance and couldn't tell them that she had her daughter with her. Oh no! She could be struggling to get the oxygen mask off, trying to tell them about me, and they would think she was just panicking because she couldn't breathe properly. Then they might give her a needle to calm her down and then she would go unconscious...I could be here all night!! Mummy, Mummy... (*She spots her.*) Oh, thank goodness! Where have you been? I've been worried sick! Don't ever wander off away from me again!

TEACHERS

Emma, Kristy and **Paige** are sitting together in the playground discussing their teachers.

Emma: I am so sick of Mrs Doolan.

Kristy & Paige: Dorky Doolan!

Emma: How's the way she gives you three seconds to get stuff out of your bag. (*She stands up and mimics her teacher.*) "Now class, you have three seconds to get your towels out of your bags. 1...2...3... last one back sees me at lunchtime!" And poor Tom was last...

Kristy & Paige: As usual.

Emma: And then she goes off at him, "Naughty, naughty, naughty, naughty boy!"

Kristy: She is soooo mean, imagine if she was your mother.

Paige: She would be like, "You have three seconds to clean your teeth and get into bed. 1...2...3!" (*They all laugh.*)

Kristy: Oh, what about Hilda High Pant!

Emma & Paige: Who?

Kristy: Miss Harrington. She wears her pants right up here. (*Pulls her skirt up to her chest and walks funny.*) She talks sooo slow!

Paige: How's the way she goes 'tsk' after every word she says. "Now hello class, tsk, today we might do some dancing, tsk."

Kristy: (*Gets up and acts out Miss Harrington.*) "Now, tsk, place your arms like this, tsk, and spin!"

Emma: Imagine if the school was on fire. We'd all be burnt to a crisp by the time she told us what to do. "Now class, tsk, keep calm, tsk, now what we're going to dooo, tsk, is file out in pairs, tsk, slooowly and calmly."

Paige: Mrs Doolan would be like, "You have three seconds before you are burnt to death. Now out of the class quick, quick, quick, quick! Tom, stay behind for being such a naughty, naughty, naughty, naughty boy!"

Kristy: I bet Miss Harrington...

Emma & Paige: (*The girls butt in.*) Hilda High Pant!

Kristy: ...would try to chat up the firemen.

Emma: Oh yeah she would!

Kristy: She would be all like, "Hi boys, tsk, ooh you're so brave. Tsk, and don't you look fancy in your uniforms, tsk."

Paige: Do you think she has a boyfriend?

Kristy: No way, she's such a dork!

Emma: Yes way! I saw her last week with a wrinkly old man, wearing those great big geeky glasses.

Kristy: It was probably her father! (*They all laugh and the lunch bell rings.*)

Paige: Oh no, now we've got Dorky Doolan all afternoon!

Emma: (*Mimicking Mrs Doolan.*) "Come on girls, quickly now, three seconds to get to class. 1…2…3!" (*They all exit laughing.*)

TEACHERS

Monologue for a young girl

I am so sick of Mrs Doolan. Dorky Doolan! How's the way she gives you three seconds to get stuff out of your bag. "Now class you have three seconds to get your towels out of your bags. 1...2...3...last one back sees me at lunchtime!"

And poor Tom was last...as usual. And then she goes off at him, "Naughty, naughty, naughty, naughty boy!"

She is soooo mean, imagine if she was your mother. She would be like, "You have three seconds to clean your teeth and get into bed. 1...2...3!"

Oh, and then there's Hilda High Pant! I mean Miss Harrington. She wears her pants right up here. And she talks sooo slow! How's the way she goes 'tsk' after every word she says. "Now hello, class, tsk, today we might do some dancing, tsk. Now, tsk, place your arms like this, tsk, and spin!"

Imagine if the school was on fire. We'd all be burnt to a crisp by the time she told us what to do. "Now class, tsk, keep calm, tsk, now what we're going to dooo, tsk, is file out in pairs, tsk, slooowly and calmly."

Mrs Doolan would be like, "You have three seconds before you are burnt to death. Now out of the class quick, quick, quick, quick! Tom, stay behind for being such a naughty, naughty, naughty, naughty boy!"

I bet Miss Harrington…Hilda High Pant…would try to chat up the firemen. Oh yeah she would! She would be all like, "Hi boys, tsk, ooh you're so brave. Tsk, and don't you look fancy in your uniforms, tsk."

I wonder if she has a boyfriend? Nah, no way, she's such a dork! Although, I saw her last week with a wrinkly old man, wearing those great big geeky glasses. It was probably her father!

Oh no, there's the bell, now we've got Dorky Doolan all afternoon! (*Mimicking Mrs Doolan.*) "Come on, girls, quickly now, three seconds to get to class. 1…2…3!"

GRANDMA'S TAPE

By Cleo Massey & Madelaine Waters

Natasha: The eldest of the two sisters. She is usually calm and controlled.
Natalie: The younger sister. Selfish and preoccupied with shopping.

Natasha is fiddling with a video camera. She puts two chairs in front of it, then goes off stage and re-enters dragging Natalie with her.

Natalie: Uhhh! What a waste of time! I so don't want to do this!

Natasha: I don't want to do it any more than you do! We have to do it for Mum! Sit down.

Natalie: Fine! Gosh, Grandma's selfish!

Natasha: You got that right! We want to be the favourite grandchildren, don't we?

Natalie: Jess and Jacinta beat us in everything! The pie eating contest.

Natasha: The best dressed at the family reunion.

Natalie: The crab race in Fiji.

Natasha: We can't let them beat us in this! You want the money from Grandma's will, don't you?

Natalie: Yeah.

Natasha: Well stop your whinging and do it! (*Natalie rolls her eyes.*)

Natalie: Fine! (*Sighs.*) But what am I supposed to say? I haven't seen her in four years! What's she like?

Natasha: I don't know any more than you do!

Natalie: Fine, I'll talk about knitting, all grandmas like knitting.

Natasha: Just be nice! Ready and…record! (*She presses 'record' and walks over to the chairs.*)

Natalie: (*Sarcastically.*) Hi Grandma!

Natasha: Hey Gran! How are you?

Natalie: Yeah, how's your health going? Doctors haven't detected any terminal illnesses yet, have they? (*Natasha kicks Natalie.*)

Natasha: Because that would be terrible, we don't want anything like that to happen to you. So are you still the owner of your yacht club?

Natalie: You must be still reeeally busy running it because you never invite us round to your 20-room mansion.

Natasha: CUT! (*She presses 'stop' on the camera.*) Natalie! You're not even trying! I've got better things to do than this!

Natalie: And what makes you think I don't? It's not easy. (*Natasha starts talking over Natalie.*) She doesn't make any effort to see us, why can't we have a nice Grandma who gives us stuff.

Natasha: (*Overlapping Natalie.*) It's hard for me as well! Stop making out like you're the only victim. We have this Grandma and we can't change that! (*Natasha and Natalie stop.*)

Natalie: You secretly love her. (*Walking towards Natasha.*)

Natasha: Take that back! I need her money for college!

Natalie: I need her money for shopping!

Natasha: Well, sit down and try to be nice!

Natalie: Whatever!

Natasha: And don't mention terminal illnesses. (*Presses 'record'.*) Go!

Natalie: Hey Grandma! How are you? How's the house? Still own the yacht club? I've always wanted to sail on a yacht! Maybe you could take us one day! We really miss you! (*Natasha is looking angry and breathing heavily. She suddenly snaps.*)

Natasha: But that's the thing, we don't! I can't take this any more. You ugly old witch! Living up there in your mansion, watching the snow falling on your million-dollar gold-plated windows. Well here's a news flash for you, Natalie and I have been busking! Yes that's right, busking for money so we can save *up for college! That's what you have left us with. (Natasha puts her* *face up close to the camera.*) NIL! (*Natalie claps hands while Natasha is staring into mid air and breathing heavily.*)

Natalie: That was amazing! Where did that come from? You sure know how to get a point across to that old bag! Oh! Still rolling. (*She gets up and stops the camera recording.*)

Natasha: What have I done? I didn't mean that. (*She pauses.*) Well kind of, but it just came out! (*Natalie comes up to Natasha.*)

Natalie: Let's send it!

Natasha: Are you kidding me?! I want the money, we have to tape over it so no one can ever see it!

Natalie: Fine, I do want to buy those shoes I saw. (*She pauses.*) I still thought you were amazing! (*Natasha walks over and sits down.*) Since when do we busk?

Natasha: We don't, it just sounded good. Now rewind!

Natalie: Uh oh! Low battery.

Natasha: Just go get some more from the box in the kitchen! (*Natalie walks stage left and rummages through the box.*)

Natalie: I can't find them!

Natasha: Uhhh! You're hopeless. (*Natasha walks over to Natalie and retrieves the batteries.*) Wow, that was hard! (*Natalie rolls her eyes and follows her back. She* *opens the camera.*) Who took the tape out of the camera?

Natalie: Don't look at me, I was in there the whole time! (*They pause and look at each other.*)

Natalie & Natasha: MUM! (*They run out.*)

THE HAIRDRESSER

Delia: Conservative girl who just wants a trim.
Hairdresser: Ultra groovy, funky, outrageous girl in her early twenties.

Delia walks into the hair salon. The hairdresser is on the phone checking the appointment book.

Hairdresser: Let me see, Saturday morning...mmm we've got one free spot at 10am...how would that suit you? (*Pause.*) No? Okay, what about earlier...say 8am? (*Pause.*) Yes, we are very busy...(*Pause.*) Oh, I know...but you know, we are very good here...most of our *stylists* have done courses in London to keep up

87

with the latest trends. (*Delia has been looking around impatiently, then checks her watch. The hairdresser mouths to her "I'll just be a minute".*) Good... okay then, you'll take the 8am time? Lovely, see you then. (*She hangs up the phone and turns to Delia.*) Now how can I help you?

Delia: I have an 11 o'clock appointment.

Hairdresser: (*Checks her book.*) Oh, you must be Debra...do come in.

Delia: It's Delia actually.

Hairdresser: Delia, what a gorgeous name, I love it. (*Leads her to her seat.*) Now pop yourself down here. (*Puts cape around her.*)

Delia: I just wanted a trim.

Hairdresser: Trim...beautiful. (*Picks up pieces of Delia's hair.*) Can I tempt you with a look at the latest styles? (*Grabs a magazine and opens it for her.*) With your natural wave and the shape of your face we could do soooo much more.

Delia: No, just a trim.

Hairdresser: (*She shoves a magazine on Delia's lap.*) Aren't these styles just divine, don't you just love this one?

Delia: Yes, but not for me, I really just want a trim.

Hairdresser: And this colour, isn't it just to die for...?

Delia: Mmm. (*Smiles politely but not interested.*)

Hairdresser: You would just look gorgeous with this colour through your hair, Debra.

Delia: Delia!

Hairdresser: And cut it up through here a bit, with longer pieces like this…(*Picks up Delia's hair and piles it on her head pulling out bits here and there.*)

Delia: I really don't think so.

Hairdresser: (*Getting carried away with her ideas.*) And then we could add some of the blonde streaks down this side.

Delia: Not really me, I don't think.

Hairdresser: Oh Debra, it is **sooo** you!

Delia: (*Getting very angry.*) My name is Delia and I just want a trim.

Hairdresser: (*Drops her hands from Delia's head as though she has been burnt.*) Fine then…no need to snap my head off, sweetie! Just trying to bring you into line with the latest fashions. (*Starts snipping away at Delia's hair.*) Only trying to spice you up a bit (*snip, snip*). Just trying to be helpful (*snip, snip*). Add a bit of oomph into your dull little life!

Delia: (*Exclaims.*) Oh!

Hairdresser: Is there a problem?

Delia: Yes! You are the problem! For a start you have been calling me Debra when I told you my name is Delia. You haven't listened to a word I've said! I came in here for a trim and you've taken no notice of what I want. All you want to do is use me for a guinea pig so you can try out your latest styles.

Hairdresser: Fine then! (*She snips at the hair a few more times then stands back and shakes off Delia's cape.*) There we go, all trimmed up, Debra…that will be $74 thankyou! (*Delia freezes in outrage.*)

THE HAIRDRESSER

Trio version

Delia: Conservative girl who just wants a trim.
Debra: Girl who is willing to try a new style, she is a bit of a sticky beak.
Hairdresser: Ultra groovy, funky, outrageous girl in her early twenties.

Delia and Debra both enter the salon. The hairdresser is on the phone.

Delia: Hello, are you before me?

Debra: I'm not sure, I have an 11.05 appointment. What about you?

Delia: Oh mine's at 11.

Debra: They are supposed to be really good here, you know, really up with the latest styles.

Delia: Oh.

Debra: Yes, I'm going to a really important do tonight... (*Debra would go on but Delia is not interested.*)

Delia: Oh nice.

Hairdresser: Let me see, Saturday morning...mmm we've got one free spot at 10am...how would that suit you? (*Pause.*) No? Okay what about earlier...say 8am?

(*Pause.*) Yes, we are very busy...(*Pause.*) Oh I know...but you know we are very good here...most of our *stylists* have done courses in London to keep up with the latest trends. (*Delia has been looking around impatiently, then checks her watch. Debra is checking her mobile. The hairdresser mouths to both girls, "I'll just be a minute".*) Good, okay then, you'll take the 8am time? Lovely, see you then. (*She hangs up the phone and turns to the girls.*) Now how can I help you?

Delia: I have an 11 o'clock appointment.

Hairdresser: (*Checks her book.*) Oh you must be Debra, do come in.

Delia: It's Delia actually.

Debra: I'm Debra.

Delia: But my appointment is first.

Debra: It's okay, you go ahead, I don't mind. (*She sits down to wait her turn.*)

Hairdresser: Delia...what a gorgeous name, I love it. (*Leads her to her seat.*) Now pop yourself down here. (*Puts cape around her.*)

Delia: I just wanted a trim.

Hairdresser: Trim...beautiful. (*Picks up pieces of Delia's hair.*) Can I tempt you with a look at the latest styles? (*Grabs a magazine and opens it for her.*) With your natural wave and the shape of your face we could do soooo much more.

Debra: (*She is listening and butts in.*) Oh I agree, sooo much more.

Delia: No, just a trim.

Hairdresser: (*She shoves a magazine on Delia's lap.*) Aren't these styles just divine, don't you just love this one?

Delia: Yes, but not for me, I really just want a trim.

Hairdresser: And this colour…isn't it just to die for?

Debra: (*Comes and looks over her shoulder.*) Oh that's divine!!!

Delia: Mmm. (*Smiles politely but not interested.*)

Hairdresser: You would just look gorgeous with this colour through your hair, Debra.

Delia: Delia!

Debra: (*Puts her hand up amused.*) I'm Debra.

Hairdresser: And cut it up through here a bit, with longer pieces like this…(*Picks up Delia's hair and piles it on her head pulling out bits here and there.*)

Delia: I really don't think so.

Hairdresser: (*Getting carried away with her ideas. Debra watches and agrees.*) And then we could add some of the blonde streaks down this side.

Delia: Not really me, I don't think.

Hairdresser: Oh Debra, it is **sooo** you!

Delia: (*Getting very angry.*) My name is Delia and I just want a trim.

Debra: (*Mouths to the hairdresser.*) I'm Debra…

Hairdresser: (*Drops her hands from Delia's head as though she's been burnt.*) Fine then…no need to snap my head off, sweetie! Just trying to bring you into line with the latest fashions. (*Starts snipping away at Delia's hair.*) Only trying to spice you up a bit (*snip, snip*). just trying to be helpful (*snip, snip*). Add a bit of oomph into your dull little life!

Delia: (*Exclaims.*) Oh!

Hairdresser: Is there a problem?

Delia: Yes! You are the problem! For a start you have been calling me Debra when I told you my name is Delia. You haven't listened to a word I've said! I came in here for a trim and you've taken no notice of what I want. All you want to do is use me as a guinea pig so you can try out your latest styles.

Hairdresser: Fine then! (*She snips at the hair a few more times then stands back and shakes off Delia's cape.*) There we go, all trimmed up Debra…that will be $74 thankyou! (*Delia is outraged.*)

Debra: My turn! (*She plonks herself down in the chair.*)

Hairdresser: Ah…. Delia isn't it? How can I help you??!! (*Delia storms out without paying.*)

FAIRIES

Monologue for a young girl

Most people don't believe me when I tell them I see fairies. I think they're just jealous. For as long as I can remember, the fairies have been my friends. They live in the great big Poinciana tree in our front garden. Sometimes late at night when everyone is asleep they come tapping on my window. They are so beautiful! My three best friends are Goldie, Silvie and Twinkles. The clothes they wear are made from flower petals and have beautiful, sparkly dewdrops around the bottom. Their wings are silver and gold and their hair is all silky like satin. Sometimes I dress them up in my Barbie's clothes and they giggle and dance around. Do you know what their favourite food is? MILO! I give it to them for a treat.

The other night the fairies all had a dance under the Poinciana tree. It was a full moon and a ring of mushrooms had grown after the rain. It was such a magical night...until five big cockroaches spoiled the party. The fairies flew off in all directions!

My dumb brother likes cockroaches, I bet he told them about the fairies' party. He thinks I'm stupid, well I think his Action Men are stupid. At least my fairies are real.

YOUNG SUPERHEROES

Young **Superman** and Young **Batman** are chatting to each other. Schoolbags with uniforms are sitting on the ground near them.

Batman: (*Mimics a girl's voice.*) Oh Superman, you're soooo strong.

Superman: Ha, you're just jealous!

Batman: (*Girl's voice.*) Could we, like, go on a date sometime? Oh please…
Superman: Just quit it, would you!

Batman: (*Girl's voice.*) But you're so muscly and we could go flying together!!!

Superman: (*Starts laughing.*) Hey, you make a really good girl, Batman.

Batman: (*Normal voice.*) Why thankyou. But seriously, that girl we just saved totally had the hots for you.

Superman: It's the suit, I tell you. Whenever I wear it I'm a chick magnet!

Batman: What can I say? I have the same problem! Man, we are just too hot!

Superman: Yeah…shame, they don't notice us when we are dressed normally.

Batman: Which reminds me, we still have to get back to school today, we have a maths test after lunch. Mum wrote me a note saying I was at the dentist this morning. What's your excuse this time?

Superman: Oh no, I forgot to get a note. Do you think we can forge one?

Batman: Hey, I can scale walls, fly through the air, catch baddies with my bare hands, but forging a note??? I don't know…

Superman: Well I can't tell the truth, can I? Hey Miss, sorry I'm late, I just used my x-ray vision to find a girl in distress at the hands of a criminal who I disabled with my iron fists.

Batman: You forgot the part where your trusty friend Batman lassoed his accomplice and distracted the others while you flew the girl to safety!

Superman: Yeah, well, don't think that story is gonna cut it. I need to forge a note.

Batman: Here's a pen and paper. (*He hands them to Superman and starts reciting.*) Dear Miss Brown, I'm sorry Clark is late today, he was delayed by a really hot girl!!! (*He starts laughing.*)

Superman: You're not helping!

Batman: Ok, ok...I'll be serious...I'm sorry Clark is late today, he was delayed when he fell ill after coming in contact with Kryptonite! (*He bursts out laughing again.*)

Superman: You're sooo funny!

Batman: I know, I know...Clark is late today as he had to help Batman, that handsome caped crusader, put a criminal in jail!

Superman: Yeah right, she'll believe that one!

Batman: Well it's the truth!...I am handsome!

Superman: Aaagh, I give up, you're no help! I'll just say I had to go to the optometrist for a new pair of glasses.

Batman: Yeah, your x-ray vision has been playing up!

Superman: No! Normal glasses for Clark, not Superman!

Batman: I'm kidding! Lighten up, would you?

Superman: (*Finishes off the note.*) Ok. Done. We better go get out of these costumes and get to school.

Batman: Shall we take the Batmobile?

Superman: No! (*Shakes his head in disbelief.*)

Batman: You wanna fly then? (*Superman shakes his head.*) Aw, come on…

Superman: (*Still shaking his head as they start to exit.*) Are you ever going to grow up?

Batman: Please? Oh come on, it's more fun than walking…Batmobile? Yeah? I'll let you drive…

FIRST LOVE

Monologue for a 12-year-old boy

Her name is Monique! Even her name is beautiful. Monique…it sounds so…I don't know, exotic or something. She is nearly 13, the same as me. She's got long chocolate brown hair and huge big hazel eyes with the longest eyelashes I've ever seen. My sister says she wears mascara, but I think they are naturally long. My sister, Jade, is best friends with Monique's little sister. That's how I met her. We had to pick up Jade from a party and Monique opened the door. I was speechless! I've never done that before. Usually I don't look twice at girls but that day, Saturday 16 May 2009, will be forever stamped in my brain. That is the day I think I fell in love. I can't believe I said that! How corny! But I tell you, I have never felt like this before. There's no way I'm telling my mates.

Simmo would tease me and probably tell Monique. I can just see it now. "Hey Monique, Jason here's got the hots for you, how's about a date?" Oh God, I'd die!

And then all her girlfriends would turn to her and giggle, she would stare back at Simmo with those huge eyes and say, "Who?"

She doesn't even know I exist. It's hopeless. If this is what happens when you grow older, it stinks. This love stuff is hard work…I think I'd rather stay a kid.

SAVE THE INSECTS

Hippy : A peaceful soul who wears colourful flowing clothes and bare feet.
Geek: He wears glasses and sensible clothes. Also has a notebook and pen.

The hippy is sitting cross-legged on the grass in the park. There is a park bench nearby which the geek sits on.

Hippy: (*Sitting cross-legged on the grass meditating.*) Ohm...Ohm...

Geek: What are you doing? Is that meditating?

Hippy: (*Smiles calmly.*) Yes, would you like to try it?

Geek: No, not really my thing I don't think. I'd rather sit on the bench here, that way I won't squash any insects. (*Gets out his notebook and pen.*)

Hippy: What do you mean?

Geek: Well, if I sit down on the grass, I'll be invading the insects' space. I'd probably kill at least a dozen ants, worms, caterpillars, spiders or grasshoppers. Imagine if I jogged round the park? (*He shudders.*) Total devastation to the insect world!

Hippy: Man, I'd never thought about it like that. (*She gets up carefully and sits on the bench.*) I don't want to be responsible for killing things! I was just trying to commune with nature...you know, breathe in the air and feel the grass beneath my feet.

Geek: Well, it'd probably be best if you kept to the footpaths from now on. That way you can see the ants and other insects and avoid crushing them. Fascinating creatures they are. (*He starts writing in his notebook.*)

Hippy: What are you doing?

Geek: Studying the wildlife. I've identified at least 27 different species of insect right here in this park.

Hippy: (*Pulls her feet up off the ground.*) That many? Here, in the park?

Geek: Probably more…I've only just started this week. Fascinating!

Hippy: Well what about all the people lying on the grass and playing ball, does that affect the insects?

Geek: Of course it does. Absolutely devastating. Dozens of deaths every second.

Hippy: Oh that's terrible!

Geek: All part of the life cycle.

Hippy: But those poor ant families who will never find their brothers and sisters again, and those poor lost caterpillars who may never reach their full potential and become beautiful exotic butterflies…

Geek: Well, that's life I suppose. Fascinating, isn't it?

Hippy: Horrifying!

Geek: The circle of Life…always another to replace the one that has just been extinguished.

Hippy: But if we watched where we stepped and were more careful, all those deaths could be avoided?

Geek: I suppose so, but I don't think that will happen, do you?

Hippy: Maybe if more people realised…?

Geek: Oh my goodness, look at that! (*He notices a butterfly in the air.*) A new species of butterfly…magnificent…I haven't seen that one…oh dear, that child just hit it with the cricket bat! What a shame. (*The hippy is shocked and upset.*) I'm sure there must be another close by.

Hippy: How can you be so callous? That child just extinguished the life of a beautiful creature.

Geek: That's the cycle of life. (*Shuts his notepad and gets up to go.*) Well, I'll be off now. Nice meeting you.

Hippy: Yes, you too, it's been very educational.

Geek: Are you going now too?

Hippy: I might just sit here a while…I need to figure out a way to get out of the park without killing anything…

Geek: Oh …good luck…but I wouldn't leave it too long, the sun is setting, and that will bring out more of the worm family, crickets, moths and of course the mosquitoes. (*He walks off leaving the hippy looking perplexed.*)

I'M TELLING MUM

Courtney: 9 years old, bossy older sister.
Toby: 7 years old, little brother addicted to his Nintendo.

Toby is sitting down playing with his Nintendo when Courtney enters.

Courtney: Toby, do you want to play shops with me?

Toby: No, I'm playing with my Nintendo.

Courtney: Mum said you had to have a rest from it, 'cos you've been playing it all morning.

Toby: I'm in the middle of a game.

Courtney: Mum said you have to stop!

Toby: I want to finish this game!

Courtney: I'm telling Mum then. (*She calls out.*) Mum!

Toby: Alright, spoilsport. Gee you're a dibber dobber.

Courtney: Am not.

Toby: Are so!

Courtney: So, do you want to play shops or what?

Toby: Only if I can be the shopkeeper.

Courtney: No, I want to be the shopkeeper, you be the customer.

Toby: That's no fun though. I want to make the machine go beep.

Courtney: It's my game and I make the rules.

Toby: You always get to be the shopkeeper.

Courtney: Alright, we'll do scissor, paper, rock to decide. (*They do scissor, paper, rock and Toby wins.*)

Toby: Right, I'm the shopkeeper!

Courtney: I'm not playing then.

Toby: Courtney, that's not fair.

Courtney: (*Shrug.*) I don't care. It's my game, I get to be the shopkeeper.

Toby: Right, I'm telling Mum! (*He storms off.*)

Courtney: (*Chasing Toby.*) Alright. I was just joking. You can be the shopkeeper. Toby...

THE DIARY

Claire: 15 years old, bossy older sister.
Sarah: 13 years old.

Claire is sitting in the girls' bedroom reading her sister's diary.

Claire: Oh my God…wow…um ah…

Sarah: (*Enters the room and sees what her sister is doing.*) What do you think you're doing? Give that back. (*She tries to grab the diary but Claire is too quick and puts it behind her back.*) That's mine. Give it to me.

Claire: (*Laughing.*) Why should I?

Sarah: It's mine!

Claire: What will *you* do for *me* if I give it back?

Sarah: Why should I do anything for you? That is my private property and I want it back now! (*She waits and watches her sister who just smiles back at her.*) Right then, I'm telling Mum.

Claire: I wouldn't do that if I were you.

Sarah: Why not?

Claire: 'cos I might just have to tell her what I read in here. (*She holds the diary up.*)

Sarah: You wouldn't!

Claire: Try me! I bet she would be really interested to find out how her knitting really came off the needles. You said the cat was playing with it. What if I told her how you pulled it off because she wouldn't let you go to the movies?

Sarah: You are sooo mean.

Claire: (*She grins up at her sister.*) Also I bet she doesn't know about you smoking a cigarette with your stupid little friend Amelia!

Sarah: That is my private stuff. Give it back! (*She makes a grab for the diary but misses it.*)

Claire: Uh ah…not until you agree to do something for me.

Sarah: Like what?

Claire: Let me think…mmmm. (*She paces the room in thought.*)

Sarah: Well?

Claire: Don't rush me, little sis…(*She paces some more, thinking.*) I know! I will give you back your stupid diary if you make my bed every day and put away all my washing.

Sarah: (*Angry.*) Alright, now give me back my diary. (*Claire throws it to her and she catches it, then locks it inside a little box, putting the key in her pocket.*)

Claire: Oh, there is the little matter of me keeping my mouth shut. Now, if you don't want me to tell Mum about the knitting and the cigarettes, you're going to have to do something else for me.

Sarah: I can't believe I could have such a mean sister.

Claire: (*Shrugs.*) Some people have all the luck!

Sarah: You are sooo mean, Claire, it's no wonder you don't have any friends.

Claire: I do so.

Sarah: You so don't. Your friendships only last a few weeks until your friends find out what you're really like.

Claire: That's not true.

Sarah: It is. How come Jade won't play with you any more then?

Claire: She thinks I dobbed on her for cheating in her English test.

Sarah: You probably did.

Claire: I didn't, I swear.

Sarah: Really?

Claire: Yes, it was Monique who dobbed on her, but Jade won't believe me and now she's not talking to me.

Sarah: (*Thinks of an idea.*) If I can convince her that it was Monique who dobbed and not you, will you promise not to tell Mum about the knitting and the cigarettes?

Claire: Mmmm…that sounds fair to me. But you have to convince her, so that she rings me by…(*she looks at her watch*) 5 o'clock tonight.

Sarah: Fine then. I'll go round to Jade's house now. (*She turns to go.*) No more poking around in my stuff and you keep your mouth shut to Mum.

Claire: I won't say a word to Mum, I promise. (*Sarah goes out the door. Claire smiles to herself.*) I may however have a little word in Dad's ear when he gets home from work!

THE MANHUNT

Gertie: 82 or 83. (*She can't remember.*) Fragile with a walking stick.
Val: Nearly 85, full of life with a wicked sense of humour.
Ethel: Nearly 81. Clutches her handbag to her front, as if her life depended on it.

The three old ladies enter and sit on a bench in the park to feed the birds.

Ethel: What a lovely day to come and feed the pigeons.

Val: Just gorgeous, Ethel, just gorgeous.

Gertie: (*She sits down.*) Oh that's better. Me poor old bones get so tired these days. (*Val gives them all some bread to throw to the birds.*)

Ethel: I found a lovely new dentist last week.

Val & Gertie: Really?

Ethel: Just lovely, he gave me a new set. (*She shows her false teeth to the others with a big grin.*)

Val & Gertie: Oooh, they're nice.

Val: Different.

Gertie: Unusual.

Val: My dentist is so handsome.

Gertie: Oh you are a one, Val. Such a flirt, always were.

Val: Oh luvvy, don't let age stop ya! (*They all giggle.*) I've had five luverly husbands and since poor Cecil passed on last year…I feel the need for a new man in me life!

Ethel: Oh Val, you're nearly 85, give it up love. (*Gertie nods in agreement.*)

Val: What? Give up men?! You must be mad!

Gertie: Maybe it's time, Val…you are getting on a bit. (*Val looks horrified.*) We all are. (*Gertie and Ethel nod to each other.*)

Val: Not bloomin' likely… give up men? Never heard anything so ridiculous. You gels are younger than me, I think I need to teach you a few things.

Gertie & Ethel: Really?

Val: Really! Ethel, how old are you?

Ethel: 81 next month, Val.

Val: Pa…spring chicken! Gertie, what about you?

Gertie: Ummm…75 I think. (*The others look shocked.*) Just tricking, girls, 82…or 83...oh one or the other.

Val: Either way you're still in the race!

Gertie & Ethel: What race?

Val: We're going to have a Manhunt race!

Gertie: A Manhunt race!

Val: Yep!

Gertie: Different…

Ethel: Unusual…

Val: A Manhunt! (*She giggles, the others join in nervously.*)

Ethel: Oh I don't know…

Val: Come on gels, it'll be fun. The last to get a date has to shout the others to lunch at the RSL downtown.

Ethel & Gertie: Ooohhh.

Val: Well? What do ya reckon, gels?

Gertie: I'm in…I think.

Ethel: Oh I'd need help, my looks aren't what they used to be.

Val: Course they are, Ethel. For a start, you've got those luverly new teeth…(*Ethel beams a huge toothy grin.*) Use them and smile more. And Gertie (*she turns to Gertie*), stand up! (*Gertie struggles to a standing position leaning on her walking stick.*) I know you need that walking stick, love, but use it with pride, strut it out more. (*Gertie struts past using her walking stick like a cane. Val and Ethel clap and whistle.*)

Ethel: Oh Gertie, very dapper, a real head turner.

Val: You'll have men chasing you before you know it!

Gertie: Oooh look girls, isn't that Horace, Lionel and Bert from the bingo last week? (*They all squint to get a better look.*)

Ethel: You might be right…(*They look at each other and grin.*) Bags I get Bert!

Val: You minx, you knew I fancied his red hair! I'll go for Lionel then. If I can't have the redhead I'll go for the bald one…I do love a man with a bald head. (*They giggle.*)

Gertie: Oh Val, you're dreadful! I guess that leaves me with Horace. Oh, he has got a luverly name, hasn't he...Horace...nice.

Val: Different.

Ethel: Unusual.

Val: Well what are we waiting for girls? Come on, we're faster than they are, we haven't got a Zimmer to slow us down!

Gertie: (*They exit in a very slow rush calling after the boys.*) Yoo hoo Bert.

Val: Fancy a game of cards?

Ethel: What about a nice cup of tea?

Gertie: Oh boys...wait up.

Val: We could play strip poker, boys!

Gertie & Ethel: (*The others stop and look at her aghast.*) VAL!!

Val: Come on gels...they'll get away, we're on a Manhunt.

Ethel: Yoo Hoo Bert...

Gertie: Boys...

THE MANHUNT

Duo version

Gertie: 82 or 83. (*She can't remember.*) Fragile with a walking stick.
Val: Nearly 85, full of life with a wicked sense of humour.

The two old ladies enter and sit on a bench in the park to feed the birds.

Gertie: What a lovely day to come and feed the pigeons.

Val: Just gorgeous, Gertie, just gorgeous.

Gertie: (*She sits down.*) Oh that's better. Me poor old bones get so tired these days. (*Val gives Gertie some bread to throw to the birds.*) I found a lovely new dentist last week.

Val: Really?

Gertie: Just lovely, he gave me a new set. (*She shows Val her false teeth with a big grin.*)

Val: Oooh they're nice.

Gertie: Different.

Val: Unusual. My dentist is so handsome.

Gertie: Oh you are a one, Val. Such a flirt, always were.

Val: Oh luvvy, don't let age stop ya! (*They giggle.*) I've had five luverly husbands and since poor Cecil passed on last year... I feel the need for a new man in me life!

Gertie: Oh Val, you're nearly 85, give it up love.

Val: What? Give up men?! You must be mad!

Gertie: Maybe it's time, Val...you are getting on a bit. (*Val looks horrified.*) We both are.

Val: Not bloomin' likely... give up men? Never heard anything so ridiculous. You're younger than me, I think I need to teach you a few things.

Gertie: Really?

Val: Really! Gertie, how old are you?

Gertie: Ummm... 75 I think. (*Val looks shocked.*) Just tricking, Val, 82...or 83...oh one or the other.

Val: Pa...spring chicken! You're still in the race!

Gertie: What race?

Val: We're going to have a Manhunt race!

Gertie: A Manhunt race!

Val: Yep! (*She giggles.*) Different...

Gertie: Unusual...

Val: A Manhunt! (*She giggles, Gertie join in nervously.*)

Gertie: Oh I don't know…

Val: Come on luv, it'll be fun. The last to get a date has to shout the other to lunch at the RSL downtown.

Gertie: Ooohhh.

Val: Well? What do ya reckon, Gert?

Gertie: I'm in…I think. But…I'd need help, my looks aren't what they used to be.

Val: 'course they are, Gertie. For a start, you've got those luverly new teeth…(*Gertie beams a huge toothy grin.*) Use them and smile more. And Gertie (*she turns to Gertie*), stand up! (*Gertie struggles to a standing position leaning on her walking stick.*) I know you need that walking stick, love, but use it with pride, strut it out more. (*Gertie struts past using her walking stick like a cane. Val claps and whistles.*)

Val: Oh Gertie, very dapper, a real head turner. You'll have men chasing you before you know it!

Gertie: Oooh look, Val, isn't that Horace and Lionel from the bingo last week? (*They squint to get a better look.*)

Val: You might be right…(*They look at each other and grin.*)

Gertie: Bags I get Horace!

Val: You minx, you knew I fancied his red hair! I'll go for Lionel then. If I can't have the redhead I'll go for the bald one…I do love a man with a bald head. (*They giggle.*)

Gertie: Oh Val, you're dreadful! (*She thinks.*) Horace...oh he has got a luverly name, hasn't he...Horace...nice.

Val: Different.

Gertie: Unusual.

Val: Well what are we waiting for, Gert? Come on, we're faster than they are, we haven't got a Zimmer to slow us up!

Gertie: (*They exit in a very slow rush calling after the boys.*) Yoo hoo, Horace.

Val: Fancy a game of cards?

Gertie: Oh boys...wait up. What about a nice cup of tea?

Val: We could play strip poker, boys!

Gertie: (*Gertie stops and looks at her aghast.*) VAL!!

Val: Come on Gertie...they'll get away, we're on a Manhunt.

Gertie: Yoo hoo, Horace...

Val: Boys...

I'M ANGRY

Monologue for a young boy or girl

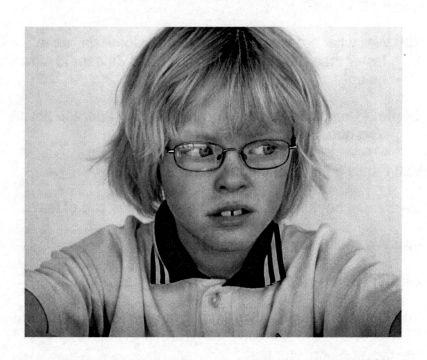

(*To his/her mother.*) Okay...deep breath...now count to ten...1,2,3,4,5,6,7,8,9,10! Nup. I'm still angry! Do it again...?

I was concentrating! Oh this is stupid! One more time then...deep breath...1,2,3,4...this is not working...5,6...it's dumb...7, 8...still angry...9,10! And hey presto...I'M STILL ANGRY!!

(*To the audience.*) I'm angry because I got sent to my room, and I got sent to my room for being angry, and I was angry because I kept getting killed on Crash Bandicoot, the PlayStation game. Mum kept saying, "Stop playing if it makes you angry, it's a game, it's supposed to be fun." She doesn't get it! Yes, it's a game, but of course you get angry if you keep getting killed and can't reach the next level!

(*To his/her mother.*) Can I come out now? Mum? MUM! I've counted to 10, can I come out now?

(*To the audience*). Oh now she won't answer me...

(*To his/her mother.*) Why won't you answer me? Now I'm getting angry all over again! MUM?! Fine then, ignore me, see if I care. I'll just stay here all night...I'll probably starve to death and you wouldn't care...(*Pause*)...I have to go to the loo...Mum, I'm busting...MUM!

(*To the audience.*) She's just ignoring me, she's probably out there having a cup of coffee and one of those new double choc Tim Tams...It's not fair...I'm getting angrier now...I want a Tim Tam.

(*To his/her mother.*) The longer you leave me here THE ANGRIER I GET. MUM!

(*Thinks a bit, then takes a deep breath.*) 1,2,3,4,5,6,7,8,9,10...(*In a nice voice.*) Mum, can I come out now?

THE DARE

Simon: 13 years old, the most sensible of the three.
Bella: Simon's mischievous 12-year-old sister.
Toby: Their 12-year-old cousin.

The three kids are sitting around at home bored, until Bella thinks up a game to entertain them all.

Simon: It's so boring, I wish we could go to the movies or to Time Zone.

Bella: Yeah, but you know what Mum would say…"Too much money!"

Toby: If we were at our farm we could go on the trail bikes, that's great fun.

Simon: Cool, I wish I'd stayed at your place this weekend instead of you coming here.

Bella: I've got an idea...but you guys might not be up for it.

Simon & Toby: What?

Bella: Well…

Simon & Toby: What?

Bella: We could give each other dares!

Toby: Oh I dunno…(*He looks at Simon to see what he thinks.*)

Simon: What sort of dares?

Bella: Last week I went to Sarah's house and she dared Emma to swim across the canal!

Toby: No way!

Simon: There's sharks in there!

Bella: Well, we don't have to do that. I'm just giving you an example. What do you think? Will we play dares… or sit and be bored?

Toby: I'm up for it. (*Toby & Bella look at Simon.*)

Simon: I suppose so…

Bella: Excellent! Who wants to go first?

Toby: What sort of things should we dare each other to do?

Bella: Anything…like…oh I know, Toby, I dare you to make a prank phone call. (*Pause, as he looks at Simon who shrugs.*) You have to say whether you'll do it or not.

Toby: (*Grinning.*) Okay I'll do it!

Simon: Here you go, here's the phone. (*Hands him the phone.*) Just make up a number. (*Toby dials a number. They are all grinning.*)

Bella: (*Whispers.*) Is it ringing?

Toby: (*Toby nods, then starts talking in a man's voice.*) Good afternoon, Madam. This is Peter Smythe from Energex. A few people in your area are experiencing problems with their power. Could you please check for me and see if your fridge is running? (*He waits a while; they are all trying not to laugh.*) It is? Well you better go catch it before it runs out the door! (*He hangs up and they crack up laughing.*)

Bella: That was hilarious. Give me a dare next.

Simon: Okay…I dare you to go knock on Cranky Bill's house over the road and then run away.

Bella: What if he catches me? Mum and Dad will freak!

Simon: You better be quick then…(*In a serious voice.*) Bella…do you accept your dare?

Bella: (*Thinking.*) Oh alright. You watch out the window. (*She goes out and the boys rush to the window to watch.*)

Toby: That was a mean one, Simon, what if he catches her?

Simon: He won't, she's fast. Oh look, she's about to ring the doorbell.

Toby: She did it, run Bella. I can't see Cranky Bill, can you?

Simon: No, not yet. Quick Bella, run. (*They are both laughing as Bella bursts in and runs to the window.*)

Bella: Is he there yet?

Toby: Yep, look, the door's opening.

Simon: He's looking around…(*They hold their breath.*) You're safe, he's given up.

Bella: My heart is beating so fast. Okay, Simon, it's your turn.

Toby: I dare you to call a taxi to Cranky Bill's house. We can watch from the window.

Bella: Oh yeah, come on Simon, it'll be hilarious.

Simon: Right, you're on. (*He grabs the phone and dials.*) Hello, could I have a taxi to...(*Bella signs the house number to him*)...35 Vermont Drive please? Yes, straight away thanks, going to?? (*He looks at the others perplexed.*) The airport! (*Pause.*) Okay thanks.

Toby: How long will they be?

Simon: They're only around the corner on the Highway, should be here any minute. (*They run to the window.*)

Bella: This is fun.

Toby: Beats being stuck on the farm. (*They laugh.*)

Bella: He'll probably be ages.

Toby: Mum always says you can never get a taxi when you need one.

Simon: Look it's here already. (*They crowd round the window.*)

Bella: Wonder what Cranky Bill will say? (*She imitates him.*) "I didn't order a blooming taxi!"

Simon: Look, he's answering the door...

Toby: He looks furious. Bella, get back he'll see you.

Simon: Oh no, he's pointing over here!

Toby: We're sprung!

Bella: Quick, let's hide.

Simon: Dur Bella, Mum will find us…quick let's get out of here. We'll go out the back way to the park.

Toby: (*Looks out the window one more time.*) Quick! They're coming over here and they look furious.

Bella: Run… (*They all run offstage.*)

MY ANNOYING BROTHER

by Cleo Massey

Monologue for a young girl

Here I am in my room. Why, you may ask? Because of two very simple and disgusting words "My Brother". I am always in my room now because of "it".

Last week we were in the car and my favourite song came on the radio. But then "it" interrupted, "Mummy, listen to this song I learnt at kindy," and started singing out loudly.

I couldn't hear a thing. "Joey be quiet or else…"

"Cleo, don't speak like that to your brother, he's trying to sing a song he learnt today."

"MUM, I WANT TO LISTEN TO THE SONG THAT'S ON THE RADIO."

Joey then looked at me with a sad puppy dog face, and Mum said, "Cleo, you can go to your room when we get home."

"Aarrrhhhhhhhhh."

When we got home I decided to try and make Mum forget, but no, Joey had to remind her. So then of course I got sent to my room for nothing once again! Which brings me to today. Half an hour ago, I was in the lounge, being a perfectly normal person watching TV, when "it" came along. "I want to watch 'Play School' Cle."

"Well *I* am watching something else, Joey."

"But Cle, I want to watch 'Play School'."

"Do you think I care? *Now go away*, I'm trying to watch TV."

So he did go away, which was very unusual. Then Mum came in. NOT good! I thought it was a bit unusual that Joey went away when I told him to. "Cleo, why won't you let Joey watch 'Play School'?"

"I want to watch this."

"Well you can't. Let Joey watch 'Play School', NOW."

So I got up to go out and as I walked past Joey, he all of a sudden started a very obvious fake cry. Then Mum starts yelling at me, "What did you do?"

"Nothing Mum. He's just faking."

"Go to your room right now!"

And that's where I am now...Hang on, I can hear Joey talking to Mum...he's probably making up something else I didn't do...no he's not, he's asking Mum if I can come out of my room now! That's weird...maybe he's not that bad after all?

ANYTHING YOU CAN DO

Two young boys are playing together and trying to outdo each other.

Joey: Hey, did you see Tony Hawk do that mega trick on TV last night?

Jordan: What mega trick? The ollie?

Joey: No, he did this flip off a staircase into a grind plus a handstand!

Jordan: Oh that...yeah, my dad can do that.

Joey: Cannot!

Jordan: Can so!

Joey: Right, then I'm gonna ask him when he comes over to pick you up.

Jordan: Well he can't do it anymore, but he did when he was younger.

Joey: This kid at school, his dad is in the Krusty Demons.

Jordan: I know that kid.

Joey: No you don't, he goes to my school, not yours.

Jordan: Yeah but I saw him once at the shop and talked to him. Anyway my mum used to go out with Robbie Williams!

Joey: Robbie Williams, the singer? Did not!

Jordan: Did so! He could have been my father!

Joey: He lives in England!

Jordan: Oh...maybe it was another Robbie Williams.

Joey: Hey, guess what? I'm going to Movie World tomorrow and I'm gonna meet Batman.

Jordan: He's not the real Batman.

Joey: Is so, and I'm gonna talk to him and ask if I can be in his next movie.

Jordan: I wish I could be in it too.

Joey: Do you want me to ask him for you?

Jordan: Yeah!!

Joey: Okay, but don't tell anyone else or everyone will want to do it.

Jordan: Cool. Hey let's go tell Jaiden that we're gonna be in a Batman movie, he'll be so jealous.

Joey: Yeah, come on then! Hey Jaiden, guess what?? (*They exit.*)

LET'S PRETEND

Rose and **Tegan** are two 7 year olds playing together.

Rose: (*Looking at a few CDs.*) Hey, let's make up a play.

Tegan: Yeah, what can we do?

Rose: Well let's pretend I'm your big sister and I'm 12…

Tegan: Okay, I'll be five then.

Rose: And my name is Britney. (*Holds up a Britney Spears CD.*)

Tegan: No, I want to be Britney.

Rose: No, I bagsed it first. You be Kylie or Miley.

Tegan: I know, I'll be Delta.

Rose: And let's make out that you keep annoying me and taking my CDs?

Tegan: Yeah and then I can run away with them. (*She grabs the CDs and runs across stage.*) And you get really mad at me.

Rose: Alright and let's make out that you fall over in the mud…

Tegan: (*Tegan slips down to the floor.*) Yeah and I get all dirty and I wreck the CDs, so you start yelling at me.

Rose: Hey and then let's pretend that I fall in the mud too!! (*She crosses to Tegan and slips down to the ground giggling.*)

Tegan: (*Laughing.*) And then we both have mud all over us.

Rose: And we start throwing it at each other. (*Both girls laugh and pretend to throw mud at each other.*)

Tegan: Then let's pretend we get scared 'cos we're so dirty and our mums will be cross with us.

Rose: Yeah so then we have to try and wash it off with a towel that we find. (*They pretend to scrub off the mud.*)

Tegan: And then we see a monster coming to get us! (*Getting excited.*)

Rose: Yeah and we try to hide 'cos we're so scared! (*They both crouch down scared.*)

Tegan: And let's pretend it chases us back in the mud again!

Rose: Yeah that will be so funny. Will we do it from the beginning now?

Tegan: Na...I'm sick of it, let's do something else!

THE NUNS

Monologue for a girl

Sister Ursula is like this old, old, old nun who teaches me piano on Mondays after school. She wears the whole, full black habit, so all you can see is her crinkly old face and pointy claw-like hands. The rosary beads around her waist rattle whenever she moves.

Usually five minutes into the lesson – around the scale of F – she falls asleep. The first time I had no idea, because she sits kind of behind me and to the right. But this day when I finished the F scale I noticed this kind of strange snorting sound. I thought it was my friends, who were waiting outside, being stupid, then I noticed it was coming from behind me. I turned around and there's Sister Ursula with her head drooped down on her chest SNORING! I didn't know whether to be insulted or to laugh. I decided to test her to see if she really was asleep, so I started the G scale and played heaps of wrong notes. She just kept on snoring. It's no wonder I can't get past grade 2 in piano.

Sister Lucy is another nun at our school. She's Irish and is famous for the 'pick it and flick it' routine. Yep...she picks her nose when she thinks we're not watching and then flicks it off her fingers. It's disgusting. We're all wise to it now and we quickly pull up our desk lids to cover us when she starts to flick.

Then there's Sister Xavier, she's an old dear, but boy, does she have a problem with wind. (*She fans her face with her hand.*) Woooo. She collects stamps so if you get her talking about your aunt who sent you a postcard from Jamaica and describe the stamp on the letter, you can miss a good 15 minutes of Maths. We take it in turns to invent relatives in exotic locations.

The nastiest of them all is Sister Vincent! She wields the ruler and slaps you round the back of the legs with it. We must have all said good prayers this year because she got transferred to another school last term.

Sister Joseph takes the cake though, she gave us the dreaded SEX talk last week. Like she would know anything about it! She's a nun!!! Anyway, all I learned from her talk is that when we get changed for sport we have to be modest and crouch down behind our desks, and if we wear a bikini we will burn in Hell!

IT'S JUST A GAME!

Jake is sitting down playing PlayStation.
Mum is reading a magazine.

Jake: Ha ha gotcha!…Yeah take that!…Ahhh…oh no!…Bam!…Nooooo…Oh unfair!

Mum: It can't hear you, Jake.

Jake: Stupid thing. I just had my top score and it blew me up!

Mum: I'm sure you'll get it again.

Jake: Yeah but it took half an hour and now I have to start all over.

Mum: Well you had fun playing it for the last half hour, so now you can have another half hour of fun.

Jake: But Mum, I just wasted all that time 'cos now my score has gone!

Mum: So do it again. It wasn't a half hour wasted, you were playing.

Jake: Oh never mind, you just don't get it, do you?

Mum: Apparently not!

Jake: (*Starts playing again, but is very grumpy.*) Take that…yeah…YES!! Come on…come on…No! No!! Stupid thing.

135

Mum: Jake, it's just a game.

Jake: This is not working properly.

Mum: A bad workman blames his tools.

Jake: There are no tools, Mum, it's a racing car.

Mum: (*Mum shakes her head.*)

Jake: Turn, turn…yes…about time…NOOOOOOOO! (*He stands up.*) Dumb, stupid game!!

Mum: That's enough, Jake. It's a game.

Jake: Well it's a stupid game!

Mum: No, you're stupid if you let it make you angry. You're supposed to enjoy playing it.

Jake: (*Trying to play one more time.*) Go…come on...yes…turn, turn, TURN! Stupid thing!

Mum: That's it. (*She gets up and takes it off him.*) No more, this is ridiculous.

Jake: Mum, now you've lost my score again!

Mum: Too bad, you're not playing it anymore until you calm down. Now go to your room.

Jake: I'm not a baby!

Mum: Then don't act like one. This is a game (*she gestures to the PlayStation*) and you're yelling at it. Go to your room until you calm down.

Jake: This is stupid!

Mum: I agree! (*Jake storms out of the room. Mum watches him go then looks at the PlayStation, sits down, checks to see that Jake is gone, then starts playing.*) Yes…woo hoo…oh no…ha ha gotcha…Oh yes I am good!!! (*She turns it off and walks out.*)

BUSH ADVENTURES

Tim: The most sensible of the three boys.
Chris: Tim and Greg have come to his house to play so he is showing them round.
Greg: Likes to think that he is the leader of the group and not Tim.

The three boys are exploring in the bush near Chris' house.

Tim: I've never been this far down the back of your house, Chris.

Chris: I have, our property goes for miles this way, right down to the creek. (*He points.*) See? (*The other boys look where he is pointing.*)

Greg: Wow you're so lucky. Our house is just in a normal old street with other houses all around us.

Chris: Do you wanna build a fort here?

Tim: Yeah, that would be cool. Let's get some sticks and logs.

Greg: There's a bunch of wood over here. (*The boys go to where Greg pointed.*)

Chris: Here, help me lift this big log. (*Greg helps while Tim looks under the log.*)

Tim: Hey wait…there's something under here.

Greg: What is it?

Tim: It's a bag or something. Keep pulling the log and I'll get it. (*Tim pulls the bag free.*)

Chris: Woh, what's in it?

Tim: I dunno. (*He unzips the bag and pulls out a wallet.*)

Greg: Show me. (*Tim hands him the wallet which he opens.*)

Tim: Is there any money in it?

Greg: (*Pulls out a wad of bills.*) WOW! Look at this!

Chris: (*Grabs some.*) Cool, think what we can buy with this.

Tim: We can't keep it. What if the owner comes back for it?

Chris: Pretty dumb place to leave your money!

Tim: Is there a name in the wallet?

Greg: (*Looks through the wallet.*) I can't see one.

Chris: Look in the bag.

Tim: Here, give it to me. (*He grabs the bag and looks through it, pulling out items as he speaks. They are all black.*) Shirt, a hat, gloves, pants…poo they stink! (*Flicks them at the other boys who shove them away laughing.*)

Greg: Er yuk!

Chris: Pooooey!

Tim: (*Suddenly becomes serious as he pulls out a knife.*) Guys…look at this!

Chris: Woh!

Greg: That is a serious knife, dude!

Tim: I'm starting to get a bad feeling about this.

Chris: Why? This is cool. We can cut sticks with the knife and make a really cool fort, then use the money to buy some toys!

Greg: Think about it, Chris! Black clothes, loads of money, a knife?!

Tim: I think this bag belongs to a robber!

Greg: (*Greg nods.*) What if he hid it and is going to come back for it?

Chris: Let's take it up to the house then and show Dad.

Greg: Good idea.

Tim: Sssh. What was that?

Chris: What?

Greg: I heard it too. Listen…I think someone's coming. (*They look at each other scared.*)

Chris: (*Whispers to the others.*) Quick, grab the bag and follow me. (*They sneak offstage quickly and quietly.*)

WOOPSIES

Monologue for a young boy or girl

Oh poo, something stinks in here. Mum is gonna have a fit, what is it??? (*Wanders to the side.*) I think it's coming from over here? Nuh. Maybe over there? (*Walks to the other side.*) Oh man!!! It's everywhere. I think the dog's done a woopsie in here somewhere. I better find it or Mum will rub his nose in it. (*Sniffs the air and wanders around looking.*)

We had the carpets cleaned last week, she is definitely not going to be happy. We had to move all the furniture and stay out of the house for the whole day waiting for the carpet to dry.

Dad and I really wanted the dog but he's not very well trained yet. Mum and my sister wanted a cat! (*Rolls eyes.*) Dogs are much more fun.

Oh it really stinks...where can it be? Uh oh, Mum's coming...(*Looks up at mother.*) Hi Mum...yeah I can smell it too. I dunno where it's coming from. I've looked everywhere. What??? (*Looks down at shoes, lifts feet and looks at shoe, then up to the mother.*)

Woopsies...

GOLDILOCKS??!!

Jess: 10 to 12 years old. She is a bit prim and sensible.
Goldilocks: 10 to15 years old, vain, bossy and not
particularly nice.

Jess is reading from a fairytale book when Goldilocks
suddenly appears with golden locks and full fairytale
costume.

Jess: "Goldilocks saw that the door to the cottage was not
locked so she opened it and went inside." Gosh I'd
never do that! "On the kitchen table were three bowls of
porridge. She tried the first one…too salty. She tried
the second one…too sweet." Oh, now her germs will be

on all the spoons! "She tried the third one...it was just right, so she gobbled it all up." Oh poor baby bear, he'll have nothing to eat!

Goldilocks: (*All of a sudden Goldilocks appears in front of Jess.*) Would you quit picking on everything I do!

Jess: (*She is in shock.*) What...? Are you...? How did you...?

Goldilocks: Yes I'm Goldilocks and I couldn't stand listening to you reading this story a moment longer. Pick, pick, pick. Can't you just read the story and leave off all the comments? Who died and left you in charge?!

Jess: Um sorry...I didn't know you could hear me.

Goldilocks: So does that make it alright, does it? It's okay to pick on people as long as they don't know about it? Lovely!

Jess: Well, no, I didn't mean that, it's just that...well...you're not real, are you?

Goldilocks: Do I look real to you?

Jess: (*Nods her head, still in shock.*) Yes.

Goldilocks: Alright then! (*She walks round the room.*) So, this is your room is it? Mmmm, you've got a lot of stuff. (*Picks up a little trinket.*) This is nice, can I have it?

Jess: What?? No. My grandmother gave it to me. Could you put it back down? (*Goldilocks glares at her.*) Please?

Goldilocks: Oh I like this dress. (*Picks one off the chair.*) This would look great on me.

Jess: Well you're not having it. It's new, Mum bought it for me and I haven't even worn it yet!

Goldilocks: (*Mimicking Jess.*) "It's new, Mum bought it for me and I haven't even worn it yet!" Wah wah. You don't like to share, do you?

Jess: Well from what I've read about you, you just take whatever you want!

Goldilocks: What do you mean by that?

Jess: Well you just broke into the three bears' house...

Goldilocks: Technically, I didn't break in because they left the door unlocked.

Jess: Whatever...you still entered a house uninvited, then proceeded to eat all their food.

Goldilocks: Hey, I was hungry!

Jess: And from what I've heard you went on to destroy their property.

Goldilocks: (*Mimics her again.*) "Went on to destroy their property..." Oh puh-leaze. It's not my fault if the stupid chair broke.

Jess: Well, did you think about how baby bear would feel when he saw it?

Goldilocks: Nuh. I'm sure he'll get over it.

Jess: You're really not very nice, are you?

Goldilocks: Never really thought about it...I have really nice hair though, don't you think? Everyone comments on it. That's why I'm called Goldilocks. (*She pauses and waits for a reaction.*) Get it?

Jess: Yeah I get it, I'm not stupid!

Goldilocks: Oooh ...I think you might be a teensy bit jealous of my beautiful golden locks.

Jess: You are so vain!

Goldilocks: And you are so plain!

Jess: I think it's time for you to go. I didn't invite you here, so I'd like you to leave.

Goldilocks: Nuh, I think I might stick around a bit, check out your house, meet the neighbours...any cute boys live nearby?

Jess: (*Realises she is going to have to trick Goldilocks to get her back into the book.*) No. No cute boys here...but you do get to meet a cute boy in your book. But I guess that won't happen if you insist on staying here.

Goldilocks: A cute boy? In my book? You're making that up.

Jess: (*Holds the book to her chest.*) No I'm not. His name is Jack and he's the woodchopper's son. He comes along and saves you from the bears.

145

Goldilocks: Does not! You're making that up. Let me see. (*Tries to get the book.*)

Jess: Uh uh. You can't see it yet because you're not in the book, you're here, so it won't show up.

Goldilocks: Are you making this up?

Jess: Why would I do that?

Goldilocks: So what does he look like...this Jack guy?

Jess: Cute.

Goldilocks: Really cute?

Jess: Extremely cute.

Goldilocks: Hair?

Jess: Curly and brown with blonde highlights.

Goldilocks: Eyes?

Jess: Sparkly green with beautiful long eyelashes.

Goldilocks: But he's poor...he's the woodchopper's son!

Jess: Oh no, but he finds out he's actually a prince and the woodchopper has been hiding him to keep him safe from the evil wizard, until he takes his rightful place on the throne. With you beside him as the queen of course.

Goldilocks: You're making this up.

Jess: Uh uh...my favourite part is when you faint after he rescues you from the bears...and he wakes you with a kiss!

Goldilocks: Alright, alright, I believe you. Stand back, I'm going back into the book. (*She jumps into the book calling out as she goes.*) Jack, Jack, I'm here...

Jess: (*Slams the book shut.*) Thank goodness. Gosh, she was the most gullible, stupid, vain girl I've ever met! I hope the bears eat her up!

EISTEDDFODS

Monologue for a young girl

Lara Falkner is always, always, always going to win, no matter what I do. Mum says it doesn't matter, "just have fun performing". But Lara will have a full sparkly costume and ringlets in her hair. Mum says she wears too much makeup and it's a disgrace to dress an 8 year old in high heels and fishnets. I think she looks like a Bratz doll. I look like a cabbage patch doll!!

Oh there she is…even her hair has glitter in it!!! She's sooo sparkly!

Oh dear…she's slipped!! I think she's really hurt herself. Oh no…I think she's broken her ankle…someone's calling an ambulance.
Oh dear…looks like Lara Falkner won't be performing today…what a shame.

RICH AND FAMOUS

Maddy and **Nicole** are two young girls talking about what they will be when they grow up.

Maddy: When I grow up I'm going to be a famous actress and singer and live in a beautiful mansion with a big long driveway and a huge pool in the garden.

Nicole: Wicked! So am I! We could be famous together!

Maddy: Yeah, we could have sooo much fun.

Nicole: We could be a girl group called… (*thinks*) "Chickie Babes".

Maddy: Or "Hot stuff".

Nicole: What about "The Cool Kids"?

Maddy: Yeah but we won't be kids then, we'll be grown-ups.

Nicole: I know…"The Cool Sisters"!

Maddy: Yeah "The Cool Sisters"! And people will come and see us from all over the world.

Nicole: We'll sing all the cool songs like Beyonce's "Single Ladies" song. (*They sing a bit of "Single Ladies" 'If you like it then you shoulda put a ring on it…oh oh oh oh oh oh…'*)

Maddy: People will throw money and flowers on stage for us. (*They act out picking up money and flowers and* *blowing kisses to the audience, saying 'thankyou' and 'you're so kind'.)*

Nicole: We'll have such huge parties at our mansion and everyone who's anyone will be there.

Maddy: *(Acting out that she is talking to these people.)* Oh Elle, how lovely of you to come…and Oprah, I didn't think you'd make it…

Nicole: *(Joins in.)* Oh look, Madonna and Britney have made it after all. And there's my namesake Nicole Kidman… can I get you a champagne? *(They both giggle.)*

Maddy: *(Mock horror.)* Surely that's not Danni Minogue over there, I didn't think she'd show her face around here!

Nicole: *(Reverting to herself again.)* I saw a TV show about her the other night.

Maddy: Me too! They said she had all these operations on her face.

Nicole: When we are rich and famous we'll have to do that too!

Maddy: No way!

Nicole: You have to. Everyone does. Or they look too old! *And* they have nannies for their children.

Maddy: *(Horrified.)* I don't want to have nannies. I want to look after my own children.

Nicole: You can't when you're rich and famous, there's no time. You will always be at concerts and movie sets and having your hair and makeup done.

Maddy: Oh. (*Upset.*) But then when do you watch TV and play with the kids and swim in the pool and all that stuff?

Nicole: I guess you don't. (*Both girls appear thoughtful, thinking about this kind of life.*)

Maddy: I don't know if I want to be "The Cool Sisters" any more when I grow up.

Nicole: Maybe we could just do it till we're, say, 25 and then stop so we could have children and not have operations on our noses.

Maddy: I think maybe 21, because that's when my mum says she started getting old.

Nicole: 21 then. Cool!

Maddy: (*Gives Nicole a high five.*) Cool!

NERVOUS

by Cleo Massey

Monologue for a young boy or girl

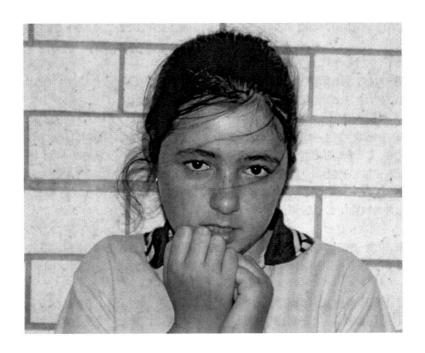

"Mum, I'm too nervous, I don't want to do it."

"You'll be great, honey."

Today is the day when I stand up on stage and do my monologue. I know I'm going to end up running off the stage sick like I did last time when all my friends were there.

"Come on, it's time to go."

"Oh great!"

When we get to the hall I see heaps of kids running over their lines and rehearsing what they have to do. "Come on, honey, let's go pay for you and get ready. Don't worry, you'll be great."

"Mum, you should have been there last time…I ran off stage sick!"

"Well you won't do it this time, will you? Okay? Let's go and watch the section before us, we're a bit early."

When we get to our seats I sit down and look up at the stage. I see a boy on stage standing still, looking like he is going to be sick. I feel so sorry for him because I know that feeling and it makes me feel worse. Then the time comes. "Your section, darling."

The first performer for my section is great! He just gets up and does it straight away. "Mum, why wasn't he nervous?"

The next performer is a little bit of a…let me say…SHOW OFF! It looks like she doesn't care what the audience thinks of her. She gets up there, waves to her mum in front of everyone and says really loudly, "That's my mum, isn't she pretty? Just like me. Everyone says good looks run in the family." Everyone is just staring at her. All of a sudden she runs off stage. Even *she* must have got scared.

"Quick, darling, it's your turn to go side stage. Good luck!"

Uh oh. This is the part where I get really nervous. Right now I'm walking up to side stage. Okay, now I'm side stage.

(*Turns around like she's going to be sick.*) Wait a minute...I'm not going to be sick...I feel great! I'm not nervous at all.

So, I walk on stage and I do my monologue. What? I'm finished already! I look at my mum and see her clapping...wait... everybody's clapping!

When I get into the car, I realise that I'm holding something. I look down and in my hand I'm holding a first place trophy!

DRESS UPS

Tara: Wants to show off to her friend Milly.
Milly: Cautious, doesn't want to get in trouble.

The two young girls sneak into Tara's mum's bedroom.

Tara: Come on Milly. (*Pause.*) It's okay, Mum is out hanging the washing.

Milly : (*Enters the bedroom.*) I don't know if I should. My mum would be really cranky if I went into her bedroom.

Tara: Oh you worry too much. Anyway I told you Mum's hanging out the washing. (*She pulls out a box of new shoes.*) Look at these.

Milly: Oh, wow! Aren't they pretty!

Tara: Mum just got them yesterday. (*She pulls them out of the box and puts them on.*) Do I look gorgeous?

Milly: Gorgeous! (*She spies some other heels by the cupboard.*) Do you think I could wear these?

Tara: Sure you can! Show me? (*Milly puts them on and struts around.*) Oooh, very fancy.

Milly: I think I need a scarf. (*She gets one off a hatstand and puts it on, grabbing another for Tara.*) Here you go.

Tara: Very special. All ladies need lipstick though. (*She gets some off the dressing table and they both put it on. The*

girls giggle and adopt fancy grown-up accents).
Cynthia darling, how lovely of you to come.

Milly: Oh my, Elizabeth, you look simply divine. Thanks for inviting me.

Tara: How have the children been?

Milly: Oh positively hideous! James has come down with chicken pox!

Tara: Oh you poor thing, how ghastly! Thank goodness you left him with the nanny! (*The girls crack up laughing.*)

Milly: (*Back to their normal voices.*) Have you seen how Toby Banks' mum walks when she picks him up from school?

Tara: I know. And the clothes she wears! My mum always says her skirts are too short!

Milly: Mine too! She walks like this…(*Milly wiggles across the room in her heels.*)

Tara: Yeah, and she's always flicking her hair and waving like this to the dads. (*She acts it out.*)

Milly: I heard that Toby's dad left them.

Tara: How do you know?

Milly: 'cos Mum was talking to your mum the other day in the car park and I was sitting in the car waiting for James to come down…he got kept in again!

Tara: OMG Milly! Your brother is always getting kept in!

Milly: I know, he's a ratbag!

Tara: Poor Toby. I'd hate it if my dad left us.

Milly: Yeah me too. (*She adopts grown-up voice again.*) Anyway darling, why don't we get ourselves a drinky poo?

Tara: (*Playing along.*) Oh yes darling, let's! (*Tara has her back to the door and suddenly Milly's face changes to one of fear.*) Milly, what's wrong? (*Milly points to the door and Tara turns round and says guiltily.*) Oh! Hi Mum…

Fouro version

Four young girls sneak into Tara's mum's bedroom.

Tara: Come on Milly. (*Pause.*) It's okay, Mum is out hanging the washing.

Milly : (*Enters the bedroom.*) I don't know if I should. My mum would be really cranky if I took my friends into her bedroom.

Teagan: Oh you worry too much. Anyway Tara told you her mum's hanging out the washing.

Rachel: Are you sure she won't mind?

Tara: Well she won't know, will she, 'cos she's outside! (*She pulls out a box of new shoes.*) Look at these.

Milly: Oh, wow! Aren't they pretty!

Tara: Mum just got them yesterday. (*She pulls them out of the box and puts them on.*)

Teagan: They are so nice.

Tara: Do I look gorgeous?

Rachel: Gorgeous! (*She spies some other heels by the cupboard.*) Do you think I could wear these?

Tara: Sure you can! Show me? (*Rachel puts them on and struts around. The other girls help themselves to a pair each as well. They all walk around as if on the catwalk.*)

Rachel: Hey how do I look?

Teagan: Oooh very fancy. (*They all giggle.*)

Milly: I think I need a scarf. (*She gets one off a hatstand and puts it on, grabbing another for Tara.*)

Teagan: Ooh me too. Here you go, Rachel. (*She passes one to Rachel.*)

Tara: Very special. All ladies need lipstick though. (*She gets some off the dressing table and they all put it on.*)

Milly: Oh I like the pink.

Teagan: Me too, can I borrow that one?

Tara: Here Rachel, let me fix yours, it's all crooked.

Rachel: Well I obviously need more practice! (*The girls giggle and adopt fancy grown-up accents.*)

Teagan: Cynthia darling, how lovely of you to come.

Milly: Oh my, Elizabeth, you look simply divine. Thanks for inviting me.

Tara: How have the children been?

Milly: Oh positively hideous! James has come down with chicken pox!

Rachel: Oh you poor thing, how ghastly! Thank goodness you left him with the nanny! (*The girls crack up laughing.*)

Milly: (*Back to their normal voices.*) Have you seen how Toby Banks' mum walks when she picks him up from school?

Tara: I know. And the clothes she wears! My mum always says her skirts are too short!

Rachel: Mine too! She walks like this...(*Rachel wiggles across the room in her heels.*)

Teagan: Yeah, and she's always flicking her hair and waving like this to the dads. (*She acts it out.*)

Milly: I heard that Toby's dad left them.

Rachel: Really? When?

Milly: Last month.

Teagan: Are you sure?

Tara: How do you know?

Milly: 'cos Mum was talking to your mum (*she looks at Tara*) the other day in the car park and I was sitting in the car waiting for James to come down...he got kept in again!

Rachel: OMG Milly! Your brother is always getting kept in!

Milly: I know, he's a ratbag!

Teagan: Poor Toby. I'd hate it if my dad left us.

160

Tara: Yeah, me too.

Milly: (*She adopts grown-up voice again.*) Anyway, darling, why don't we get ourselves a drinky poo?

Teagan: Do you think we should???

Tara: (*Playing along.*) Oh yes, darling, let's! (*Tara has her back to the door and suddenly Milly's face changes to one of fear.*) Milly, what's wrong? (*Milly points to the door and Tara turns round and says guiltily.*) Oh! Hi Mum...

THE SOLAR SYSTEM RAP

Up in the solar system out in space

There are nine planets that I had to trace

For a poster, to put up on the wall

But I kept on forgetting, couldn't remember them all

So I made up a line using all the first letters

My **V**ery **E**nglish **M**other **J**ust **S**ent **U**s **N**ine **P**resents

Mercury, Venus, Earth and Mars

Jupiter and Saturn are near the stars

Uranus, Neptune, then the coldest one

Pluto, is blue, the furthest from the sun

Now remember the line using all the first letters

My **V**ery **E**nglish **M**other **J**ust **S**ent **U**s **N**ine **P**resents

CHRISTMAS RAP

Yo, listen up dudes, I'll tell it to you straight

It's Christmas soon, so it's not too late

To start being nice and kind and good

So you get lots of presents like you think you should

Yo, the big fat dude with the beard of white

Won't pull any punches in the dead of night

He'll skip your house if he thinks you've been bad

On Christmas day your face will be sad

When you search through the presents and there's none for you

You'll wish that you hadn't been naughty and rude

Don't spit the dummy! Smile heaps, don't shout!

Be good and kind, don't frown and pout!

Santa likes kids who are happy not grumpy

And he'll fill their stockings till they're fat and lumpy!

School Stuff For Kids To Perform

This section includes various scripts involving the same characters. The characters are all students at the same secondary school. The scripts can be performed separately or in conjunction with each other.

THE GEEK

Monologue for a boy in his early teens

Sometimes I just feel like going up to him and saying, "You are the biggest, ugliest and dumbest person I know and this is for you." And then I punch him so hard in the stomach that he's winded and falls to the ground. That's when all the kids in the playground gather round and cheer me. That's what I'd like to do, but I don't have the guts. Maybe he's right, I am a puny, four-eyed geek! Even my name is wimpy...Cecil Muggeridge. Don't you laugh too! What a name to be stuck with all through life. At least the school bully has a strong name...Bruce Jones or Jonesy or Bruiser. That's what his mates call him. They all sound tough, not like Cecil!

Mum says it's a name of great historical importance. "Every first born male in the Muggeridge family has been called Cecil for seven generations."

Well, sorry to say that tradition is stopping with me. There's no way I'm going to put my kid through hell with this stupid name.

I've got to do something about my image, I'm so uncool. Sure, I wear all the name brands, it's just that none of them are NIKE, Billabong or Converse. Mum insists on Osh Kosh, Country Road and Colorado. My glasses are Pierre Cardin...how embarrassing.

And then there's our car, a vintage Jaguar! Why couldn't we have a four-wheel drive like all the cool kids. Bruce Jones's family has a red Toyota people mover! Mum says I should think myself lucky that I'm an only child instead of having seven brothers and sisters packed into a car like sardines. Sometimes, I think I'd like to be a sardine...

THE SCHOOL BUS

Madelaine and **Julia** are young girls on the school bus coming home.

Madelaine: Eeeooo, this bus stinks! (*She holds her nose.*)

Julia: It's all the smelly boys up the back. Here, let's grab these seats. (*They sit down.*)

Madelaine: Oh, I can barely breathe. (*She calls to the bus driver.*) Can you turn the air conditioner up to full please!

Julia: Madelaine! Shoosh, you'll get us kicked off the bus. Oh my God, look who just got on. (*They watch as a girl passes them.*)

Julia & Madelaine: Tiffany Golden!

Madelaine: She is so on herself!

Julia: How's the way she always waits till the last minute to get on the bus?

Madelaine: Yeah, that's just so she can walk past everyone as though she's on the catwalk!

Julia: Let's see if she sits next to Bradley…(*They turn to watch.*) Told you she would.

Madelaine: Any minute now she'll do the hair patting routine. (*She counts down as they watch.*) 5,4,3,2 and bingo! (*They both run their fingers down their hair patting it flat.*)

Julia: Now the lip gloss…wait for it…(*They both pretend to put lip gloss on.*)

Madelaine & Julia: (*They look at each other and say together.*) Beautiful!

Madelaine: Don't forget the legs. (*They turn to look at Tiffany, then both cross their legs.*)

Julia: And finally there's the girly giggle. (*They turn to watch.*) Oh, maybe she's forgotten that one.

Madelaine: No…here it comes! (*They both cover their mouths with one hand and do a fake giggle.*)

Julia: Ooh, it's so fake, it's sickening.

Madelaine: I don't know what Bradley sees in her!

Julia: Oh, all the boys are the same. They flock around her as though she was the queen.

Madelaine: I bet she'll be a weather girl when she leaves school.

Julia: She *SO* will! I can just imagine it. (*She pretends to be the weather girl.*) HI, this is Tiffany Golden with tonight's weather. (*She pats down her hair.*)

Madelaine: (*They both cross their legs.*) There has been an unexpected cold front causing showers down the east coast. So ladies don't forget your brollies as that rain can play havoc with your hair! (*They both do the fake giggle.*)

Julia: And now for a closer look at the temperatures...Brisbane warm and 29 degrees.

Madelaine: Coolangatta fine with a top of 28.

Julia & Madelaine: (*Together.*) Taree, 22. (*They both burst out laughing.*)

Julia: Hey, maybe Bradley will be the news anchor man. (*Pretending to be Bradley.*) Good evening, I'm Brad Warren, welcome to Nine Gold Coast News.

Madelaine: Tonight's headlines include a story on a local school bus. Two young girls were nearly suffocated when an air conditioner on their school bus ceased to function properly.

Julia: The girls were rushed to St Vincent's Hospital where they are reported to be in a stable condition. (*Both girls laugh.*)

Madelaine: Oh, our stop is next, quick. (They both grab their bags and run to the front of the bus.)

Julia: At last, fresh air. (*They exit taking big, exaggerated breaths.*)

THE PRINCIPAL'S OFFICE

Jonesy: Very streetwise, always in trouble.
Sasha: Nice boy with a caring family. He doesn't often get in trouble.

Jonesy is sitting outside the Principal's office looking bored when Sasha comes and joins him.

Sasha: (*Sits down and looks across at Jonesy.*) You been waiting long?

Jonesy: 'bout 10 minutes. He's in there interviewing some new kid and their parents…suckers!

170

Sasha: Oh.

Jonesy: What did you do?

Sasha: Got caught smoking…again! I think I'm in for it this time 'cos it's the second time.

Jonesy: Hey, you might get a long weekend out of it!

Sasha: What?

Jonesy: You know…get suspended for a few days. It's a nice holiday. I've been suspended twice now!

Sasha: Serious? My parents would kill me.

Jonesy: Mine don't care, they don't even notice whether I go to school or not. Half the time I just hang down the mall for the day instead of coming to school.

Sasha: Doesn't *anyone* notice?

Jonesy: Oh, every now and then. That's why I'm waiting here today. My class teacher said she wants to talk to my parents about my "frequent absences" and sent me to see the Principal. Also that geeky kid, Muggeridge, reckons I was picking on 'im.

Sasha: What are you gonna say?

Jonesy: I'll just tell them it's more fun at the mall. School is boring. And that geek needs to toughen up, he's a wimp!!

Sasha: But how are you going to get a job if you keep wagging, you'll never pass your exams?

Jonesy: Who needs a job? Only suckers work. I'll just go on the job seeker's allowance. That's what me old man does. And Mum gets heaps in child support from Centrelink.

Sasha: Don't you want to have a career though?

Jonesy: Nuh!

Sasha: I want to get a really good job where I can work my way up to be, like the head of the company or something. Then I can earn heaps and get one of those cool houses on the beach and drive a red sports car with no roof.

Jonesy: You're dreamin'.

Sasha: Yeah, of course I am. You have to dream. If you don't dream what can you look forward to?

Jonesy: Being suspended and hanging in the mall. (*He grins.*)

Sasha: That's just this week. What about next month? Next year? When you're an adult?

Jonesy: (*Shrugs.*) Don't really care that much.

Sasha: I've got it all planned out.

Jonesy: Man, you sound like a teacher! You're only 13. Live a little. Although at least you've been living a little dangerously.

Sasha: What do you mean?

Jonesy: Smoking! (*Teasing Sasha.*) Don't ya know it could give ya cancer and kill ya?

Sasha: Yeah I know. I shouldn't do it really.

Jonesy: Man you're such a dag!

Sasha: Why?

Jonesy: (*Pretending to be Sasha.*) Oh, I really shouldn't smoke it's so bad for me. You should go and chum up with Cecil Muggeridge!

Sasha: Well it is bad for you.

Jonesy: Well you're not gonna be the president of your own company if you die of lung cancer at 25, are ya? So much for ya big plans.

Sasha: You're right! (*He thinks for a minute.*) I'm gonna stop smoking as from today.

Jonesy: Betcha can't!

Sasha: I'll bet you I can. I bet you can't go a whole week at school without wagging!

Jonesy: Could if I wanted!

Sasha: Couldn't.

Jonesy: Could so!

Sasha: Prove it!

Jonesy: How?

Sasha: I'll stop smoking if you come to school every day for two weeks straight.

Jonesy: This is dumb.

Sasha: Piker!

Jonesy: Am not!

Sasha: Prove it then!

Jonesy: (*Thinks for a minute.*) Alright, you're on, but it's stupid!

Sasha: Shake on it. (*Holds out his hand, they both shake.*) Deal!

Jonesy: Dumb deal! (*Sasha smiles. Jonesy looks up as the Principal's door opens.*) Looks like it's my turn. (*Gets up to go.*)

Sasha: Remember our deal!

Jonesy: Yeah yeah…(*He walks off.*)

PRUDENCE THISTLEWHITE

Monologue for a girl in her early teens

(*Sitting alone sadly.*)

Maybe the "Populars" are right, I am a nerdy, four-eyed dag with no fashion sense! My name is 'tres' nerdy...Prudence Thistlewhite. Thistlewhite!!! For goodness sake, what a ridiculous surname and even more ridiculous when it is coupled with Prudence!

(*She stands as Tiffany walks past.*) Oh hi. (*Gives a little wave.*) Her name is sooo cool...Tiffany Golden...what a dreamy name...it's no wonder she's the most popular girl in the school, her parents gave her a fantastic name right from the start, of course she was going to grow up beautiful and popular. How could you not be beautiful and popular with a name like Tiffany Golden?? Prudence Thistlewhite! I mean puh..leaze?! What hope have I got?

Mum thinks it's a beautiful traditional name. (*Walks, whilst imitating her mother.*) "You should be thankful we didn't give you one of those stupid made up names like Tracey, Stacey, Kristy, Kirsty or Crystal. They are sooo suburban!"

(*Running across the stage.*) Oh, there she goes again, did you see her?… Tiffany Golden…she is sooo cool. And what about the dress? I'm sure it was a Bardot. That is a really, really cool brand. Mum says it's too old for me and that my Pumpkin Patch frock is much more age appropriate! OMG!!…that's what Tiffany says. It means "Oh My Gosh!" She's sooo popular. I wish I was popular. I've got to do something about my image, I'm so uncool. I'd give anything for a pair of Roxy or Billabong shorts. Mum insists on buying Country Road and Colorado because "they are quality brands".

For my birthday, I asked for a cruiser bike, you know the cool ones with the baskets that everyone has now? Mum got me a $900 mountain bike with a million gears and matching racing helmet! It's soooo embarrassing. Tiffany Golden has a pale blue cruiser with a cane basket. Sometimes she even puts her toy poodle in the basket…our Doberman is as big as my bike!!!

You know what? I've had enough! I'm going to change. I'm going to get cool. I'm going to buy some new clothes, trade in my bike for a cruiser and change my name to Pru! Look out "Populars" 'cos here I come! (*She storms off stage, tripping as she goes.*)

OMG!!!

Tiffany: Thinks she is the most popular girl in the school.
Brad: Captain of the football team, Tiffany's boyfriend.
Jonesy: Tough guy, some would call him a bully.
Prudence: Total geek.

Tiffany is sitting with Brad in the playground. Prudence is watching whilst eating her lunch. Jonesy enters a little later.

Tiffany: I'm like sooo totally going to be the hottest girl there. I have my dress picked out and I'm getting my hair done at that really expensive place at the mall, plus Daddy's paying for my spray tan and nails round the corner at "Make me a Star Boutique". Oh it's soooo exciting, Brad.

Brad: Yeah.

Tiffany: Have you picked your suit yet? We should really wear matching colours. My dress is like this beautiful shade of coral so you could like wear a tie or something in the same colour. Brad, what do you think? Brad, are you listening?

Brad: What? Oh yeah. Whatever…I just need to talk to Jonesy. (*He gets up to go as Jonesy walks towards him.*)

Jonesy: Yo Bradster.

Tiffany: But Brad…(*She pouts, then starts playing with her phone.*)

Brad: Hey Jonesy, come and save me. Man! Tiff is drivin' me nuts.

Jonesy: Yeah, girls can do that!

Brad: I dunno if I can do this school formal thing.

Jonesy: What do ya mean?

Brad: She won't stop going on about it. She wants me to wear a coral tie!

Jonesy: You cannot wear a coral tie, man! You'll never live it down.

Prudence: (*She notices Tiffany is alone and she sidles up to her.*) Hi Tiffany. That's a cool phone.

Tiffany: What? (*She looks around and calls out.*) Brad! (*He just waves her off. She looks back at Prudence who is still standing there.*) Who are you?

Prudence: Prudence…you know, Prudence Thistlewhite. I'm in your Maths class. I really love your hair colour, is it natural?

Tiffany: What?! No, of course it's not natural. You can't get hair colour like this naturally. It cost a fortune.

Prudence: Wow. You're so clever to pick it.

Tiffany: Yeah whatever. (*She starts typing on her phone and breaks a nail.*) Oh damn! Now I've broken my nail.

Prudence: Show me, maybe I can help.

Tiffany: How can you possibly help?

Prudence: I have superglue. Look, I can put a bit on the break and you can paint over it.

Tiffany: Really? Will that work? (*They start gluing the nail.*)

Jonesy: You're gonna have to dump her, man.

Brad: Yeah, I know. But how can I do that when she thinks we're going to the formal together?

Jonesy: Ya just do it! Why don't you take that Kristy Brown chick instead? She's hot.

Brad: Yeah she is, isn't she? Maybe I should just text her, that'll be easier than telling her.

Tiffany: (*Starts screaming.*) WTH?! OMG look what you've done! Now my fingers are like totally stuck to my phone!

Prudence: I told you not to touch anything till it dried.

Tiffany: Brad. Quick, help me. (*Brad and Jonesy come over to the girls.*)

Brad: What's wrong?

Prudence: I told her to let the glue dry before she touched anything.

Tiffany: Yes, but I had to check my MySpace 'cos I had a new photo on it, and I had 78 views and only five comments! Oh Brad, what will I do?

Brad: Umm, maybe some metho will soften the glue?

Jonesy: I wouldn't count on it.

Tiffany: No! I mean about my MySpace comments.

Prudence: If you add me, I'll comment you.

Tiffany: (*Looks at her in horror.*) Are you serious?

Prudence: Yes. I could say something like, 'OMG, wow Tiff, you look like a totz hot babe!'

Tiffany: Brad, get her away. I'm starting to feel ill now and I can't get my fingers off this damn phone.

Prudence: (*To Brad.*) Do you want me to take her to the office?

Jonesy: Yeah, good idea.

Tiffany: (*Screams at Brad.*) No! You take me. Get her away from me.

Brad: (*Looks at Prudence and shrugs then says to Jonesy.*) Are you coming?

Jonesy: Nah, you can have this one all to yourself, mate. I might skip this arvo and go down to the mall. Catch ya later. (*He walks off.*)

Tiffany: Brad, get me away from her. (*They start to move off, leaving Prudence on her own.*) I'm feeling faint now. OMG only five comments after 78 views…what's going on???

Prudence: Are you sure you don't want to add me? I'll leave you loads of comments. Tiff? If you change your mind just look me up...Prudence Thistlewhite. Got that? (*She spells it out.*) T.H.I.S.T.L.E.W.H.I.T.E.

 JEEPERS!

Sasha: 13 years old, nice boy but a bit of a ratbag.
Lily: 6 years old, the annoying kid sister.
Zane: 16 years old, the eldest and most responsible.

Zane is sitting in the lounge with a magazine when Sasha
and Lily come home from school.

Sasha: I'm home. Hey, where is everybody?

Zane: I'm in the lounge. Mum's not home yet, she's just
gone to get some shopping.

Sasha: Oh good then, I've got some time to figure out what
to do.

Lily: Sasha is in big trouble.

Sasha: Shut up, Lily.

Zane: What have you done this time?

Sasha: I've got a letter for Mum and Dad, but I don't know
what it says. (*Holds envelope up to the light trying to
see the contents.*) It's from the Principal.

Zane: Jeepers!!!

Lily: (*Singing.*) Sasha's in big trouble, Sasha's in big trouble.

Sasha: Lily shut up or I'll... (*He tries to grab her and Lily
hides behind Zane.*)

182

Zane: Sasha, leave her alone or you'll be in bigger trouble. Now tell me what you did.

Lily: He was smoking near the gym.

Zane: Jeepers, Sasha, you're an idiot.

Sasha: Maybe I could burn the letter?

Zane: Mum would smell it.

Lily: You could throw it in the bin?

Sasha: Dad would find it when he puts out the rubbish. (*Pause.*) I should have left it on the bus.

Zane: The bus driver would have found it and delivered it himself.

Sasha: Jeepers, what am I gonna do?

Lily: Eat it!

Sasha: Yeah right!!

Lily: No really. I've seen spies do it in movies. That's how they get rid of secret messages.

Zane: But Lily, the messages aren't usually a whole page long in an envelope.

Lily: Oh well, it was just an idea.

Sasha: What if I hide it in my room?

Zane: Mum will find it when she cleans up.

Lily: Suck it up the vacuum cleaner!!

Sasha: A dur…it's too big, it would block it up.

Zane: Jeepers Sasha, why were you smoking at school?

Lily: Sasha's in big trouble.

Sasha: Oh Zane help me, what am I gonna do???? Mum will be home any minute. (*Sound of the door opening and closing and the mother's voice; "Hi kids I'm home".*)

Sasha, Zane & Lily: (*All three look at each other and then say together.*) JEEPERS!!

TIFFANY GOLDEN

Monologue for a teenage girl

I'm Tiffany Golden, the most popular girl in the school! Why am I popular? Why do you think? I wear all the right clothes, I have gorgeous hair, I live in the best street, my parents treat me like a princess, I wouldn't be seen dead in Kmart or

Target...uhhh, I have the coolest, newest model touch screen phone, everyone's jealous...and I'm cute and funny. I know what you're thinking...God she's so vain! Well I'm not, I'm just realistic! I'm the lucky one who got all the goodies and Mum says I should be grateful that I'm so perfect! Oh I forgot, I'm also dating the biggest hunk in the school...Brad Warren, he's the football captain.

Anyway, now that you know a bit about me, you can appreciate why I'm so angry today...Kristy Brown was just voted school captain!! Kristy Brown!! For goodness sake!! Everyone knows that the students vote for the school captain and she is so *NOT* as popular as me.

Brad was voted school captain for the boys and *I* was supposed to be the girl captain. It goes without saying. We are going to the school formal together and we'll obviously get the prize for the best dressed couple. Then everything will be ruined when Kristy Brown has to get up with Brad and give a speech before supper. Everyone knows that my speeches are witty and clever. Hers will be all sensible and boring.

Oh, excuse me, my phone's buzzing. (*She gets out the phone and looks at the number.*) Whose number is that? Hello, Tiff here...oh, hi Brad, have you got a new phone number? No? Well whose phone are you using? What? Kristy's? Why? Brad? What?? You can't be serious? But Brad, it's all planned...I've already picked out my dress...Brad...you cannot seriously want to ditch *me*, the most popular girl in the school, for someone called *Brown*! Brad? Brad!! BRAD!!

He hung up on me...I can't believe it! Oh...my...God...Brad Warren, football and school captain, just dumped ME, Tiffany Golden, the most popular girl in the school, for a girl called Kristy BROWN!! Can this day get any worse...(*She storms off.*)

MYSPACE

Two teenage girls meet up in the school playground.
Madelaine is sitting down crying when **Julia** enters.

Julia: Oh there you are, Madelaine, I've been looking everywhere for you. Are you crying? What's wrong?

Madelaine: Oh you wouldn't understand.

Julia: What wouldn't I understand?

Madelaine: Well you're so popular, this sort of thing never happens to you.

Julia: What sort of thing?

Madelaine: The worst sort!

Julia: Would you stop talking nonsense and tell me what's the matter. I don't know what you're talking about.

Madelaine: Being put down to number eight is what I'm talking about!

Julia: Number eight what?!

Madelaine: Number eight on Kristy's list of Best Friends on MySpace!! Last week I was number two after you, then she moved me to four after Sarah and Josie, and now I'm number eight!!!

Julia: You don't even like Kristy!

Madelaine: That's beside the point! What will people think!?

Julia: Nothing! They will think nothing! You're still number one on *my* MySpace!

Madelaine: Thanks. You are on mine too. (*Julia starts fiddling with her phone.*) What are you doing?

Julia: Oh, just checking my messages.

Madelaine: What number am I on your speed dial?

Julia: Three? Why?

Madelaine: You're number one on mine!

Julia: You told me number three was your favourite number!

Madelaine: Yeah it is, but people will think you like your number one and two people more than me. Can you change it?

Julia: Madelaine, you're getting paranoid!

Madelaine: No I'm not. (*She gestures to Julia's phone.*) You just got a message.

Julia: Oh, it's from Kristy. (*Reading it to herself.*) She's having a party this weekend.

Madelaine: (*Gets out her phone and checks it.*) I didn't get one. Why didn't I get one?

Julia: (*Looks uncomfortable.*) Just wait a minute, maybe you'll still get it. (*They both stand looking at the phone;*

189

Madelaine checks it again.) Maybe there's no signal here, should we move away from the buildings?

Madelaine: Dur, Julia, you just got your message okay! There's nothing wrong with the signal. (*Julia looks embarrassed.*) I get it...she moved me down to number eight. It's obvious. Now I'm not in her BFF (best friends forever) group anymore!

Julia: (*Checks her phone again.*) She says it's only a small party, her parents will only let her invite seven girls and seven boys...(*She realises what she just said.*)

Madelaine: (*Starts crying again.*) That's it...I'm out of the BFFs. I'll probably be number 11 tomorrow!!

Julia: SSShhhh. (*Pats Madelaine on the knee trying to comfort her. Madelaine sees a friendship band on her wrist.*)

Madelaine: That's new. I haven't seen that friendship band before. Who gave you that one?

Julia: (*Seems embarrassed and tries to pull her hand away.*) Oh no one.

Madelaine: Kristy!!! (*Julia doesn't answer.*) Kristy gave it to you, didn't she?!

Julia: Well, I couldn't say I didn't want it, could I?

Madelaine: You don't have to wear it though!

Julia: I like it. Why shouldn't I wear it?

Madelaine: I gave you a friendship necklace. Do you still have it on?

Julia: The chain broke. I have to get it fixed. (*Madelaine looks at her in disbelief.*) It did! Dad said he'd fix it for me.

Madelaine: Oh I get it now! I'm so stupid!

Julia: What are you talking about?

Madelaine: You and Kristy, the new "Populars". I've been kicked out, haven't I? I thought *we* were best friends.

Julia: We are. I just like to hang with a group of people, not *just you* all the time.

Madelaine: I thought you liked me.

Julia: I do! I just wish you would hang out in the group though. I don't like it being just the two of us all the time, it gets boring. It's more fun to hang out with all the others as well.

Madelaine: Fine then! You go find your new BFFs. But I'd keep checking what number you are on their MySpace if I was you, because you might be number one today, but when the "Populars" are bored with you, you'll be number eight too before you know it!! (*She storms off.*)

Julia: (*Chases after her.*) Madelaine, wait…

DON'T MESS WITH THE MUMMY'S BOY

Cecil: Puny geek with glasses.
Jonesy: The school tough guy.

Cecil is sitting down reading a book when Jonesy comes up behind him and snatches it from him.

Cecil: Hey, give that back!

Jonesy: What's so important? It's just a book.

Cecil: Yeah it's mine, give it back. It's no use to you anyway.

Jonesy: Oh, think you're the only one who can read, do ya? I *can* read, ya know. (*He opens the book but struggles to read it.*) What does this stuff say? (*Pause as he tries to figure it out.*) It's not even in English.

Cecil: It's French. Can I have it back? (*He pauses and Jonesy gives him the 'say please' look.*) Please?!

Jonesy: That's all you had to say, Muggeridge. (*He gives back the book.*) Manners, manners. You gotta remember the magic word. Surely your Mummy taught you that!

Cecil: (*He mutters.*) Yeah, did yours?

Jonesy: What did you say?

Cecil: Yeah, for sure.

Jonesy: Not trying to be smart with me, are ya Muggeridge?

Cecil: Me smart? Never!

Jonesy: Yeah, well just you watch it.

Cecil: Watch what?

Jonesy: What?

Cecil: You said I should watch it.

Jonesy: Yeah, ya should.

Cecil: Should what?

Jonesy: What?! Are you trying to confuse me?

Cecil: No, you can do that all on your own.

Jonesy: Do what on my own? What are you on about? Are you saying I've got no mates?

Cecil: I don't know. Have you?

Jonesy: Have I what?

Cecil: Got any mates?

Jonesy: You better watch it, Muggeridge. I know what you're trying to do with ya smart alec words, ya big namby pamby Mummy's Boy!

Cecil: What?

Jonesy: Are ya deaf or somethink? (*He yells.*) I said I know what you're trying to do with ya smart alec words, ya big namby pamby Mummy's Boy!

Cecil: And I said what?

Jonesy: I just told you!

Cecil: (*Shakes his head in disbelief at how thick Jonesy is.*) Never mind.

Jonesy: Yeah well…you never mind either!

Cecil: Okay, I won't.

Jonesy: Good!

Cecil: Good!

Jonesy: Stop copying me.

Cecil: I'm not. I was just agreeing with you.

Jonesy: No ya wasn't. You was trying to make me look stupid again. I know your little game, Muggeridge.

Cecil: Do you?

Jonesy: Yeah!

Cecil: Okay then. Well I'm off now. (*He starts to leave.*)

Jonesy: Yeah I thought I could smell something. (*He laughs at his own little joke.*)

Cecil: Very funny. That's original, Jonesy. (*Keeps walking off.*)

Jonesy: Oi! I didn't say you could leave yet. Ya got any money?

Cecil: Are you serious?

Jonesy: Yeah I'm serious. I wanna buy a coke. Cough up.

Cecil: I'm not giving you my money.

Jonesy: Yeah ya are.

Cecil: No I'm not!

Jonesy: (*He holds up his fists threateningly.*) These little friends of mine say you are!

Cecil: I'm not giving you my money.

Jonesy: (*Jonesy hits his fists together menacingly.*) Cough up, Mummy's Boy.

Cecil: Okay. If you keep pushing me, you give me no choice. (*He strikes a karate pose and screeches like a banshee. He waves his arms round in a demented fashion screeching, while Jonesy looks on confused. All of a sudden he gives one last 'yi-hah' and runs away.*)

Jonesy: What the hell??!!! (*He looks confused then runs off after him.*)

BRAD WARREN

Monologue for a teenage boy

Geez, I'm in trouble now! No matter what I say to Tiffany it's the wrong thing. That's why I dumped her. Oh man, now she's on the rampage. Well, what did she expect? She's so bossy, always telling me what to wear and wanting me to buy her presents. I was going broke dating her! I know she's really peeved with me for dumping her before the formal. But hey, I just couldn't bear the pressure of standing up there on stage with her if we were voted best couple. Public speaking is not my strong point! And then I couldn't stand the drama if we *weren't* voted best couple! Hey, I don't need the hassles! Besides, she wanted me to wear a coral tie!!!

Kristy Brown is much easier to date...plus she totally thinks I'm the hottest guy in the school...what can I say? I love the attention! With Tiffany it was all about her, at least Kristy appreciates me. And she's pretty good looking...not as hot as Tiff but, you know, a close second. Anyway she promised she'd come to every footy game this season to watch and cheer me on. As captain of the team it's a bit lame if my girlfriend doesn't even show up to support me. Tiffany didn't like to come 'cos she said she gets mud on her shoes! Geez she was a pain. I'm well shot of her.

Hey, just thought of another bonus with Kristy...she is so smart! Like I totally suck at Maths and English...and Science...oh and I failed History last term...Anyway, Kristy said she'd help me. But I know I can scam it so that she does my assignments for me. Hey, I'm too busy with training to do them myself.

BFFLS

Kristy Brown and **Julia** are on a computer at Kristy's house. **Tiffany Golden** and **Brittany** are on another one at Tiffany's house. They are talking to each other on MySpace using all the short forms and text terms below.

Nm – never mind
g2g – gotta go
brb – be right back
atm – at the moment
msn – instant messaging
soz – sorry
fyi – for your information
lol – laugh out loud
rofl – rolling on the floor laughing
zomg – Oh My God
beb – babe
mwah – kiss
l8r – later
wth – what the hell
bffl – best friends for life
lovez ya – love you
totz – totally
ova – over
pics – pictures/photos
dp – display picture
chu – you
chyea – yeah
btw – by the way
bf – boyfriend
ur – you are

MySpace functions:
Mood – display cartoon showing how you are feeling
Default – main picture
Truth box – box on MySpace where you can anonymously
put comments

Tiffany: MySpace?

Brittany: Totz.

Tiffany: (*Signs in.*) Tiff@hotworld...godess111xxx

Brittany: Cool password.

Tiffany: Chyea.

Brittany: Why is your mood sad face?

Tiffany: A durr, Britt! Atm really down.

Brittany: Oh soz...Brad? (*Pats her shoulder.*) Nm.

Tiffany: (*She nods then types.*) Changing it to heartbroken...(*She points at the screen.*) Britty, look at my totz hot shot.

Brittany: You are sooo a beb, Tiff.

Tiffany: Comment me!

Brittany: For sure. (*Typing.*) Tiff, ZOMG ur like so hot. BFFL lovez ya beb mwah xoxo

Tiffany: Awwww sweet. ZOMG look who signed in! (*Points at screen.*)

Tiffany & Brittany: BROOOOWN!!

Kristy: Eeeeeooo, Squiffy is on!

Julia: Who?

Kristy: Tiffany!

Julia: Eeeooo! Check out the dp.

Kristy: Gay!!!

Julia: Totz! And the default!? Wth?

Kristy: Gag...ZOMG read Britt's comment.

Julia: (*Mimicking Brittany.*) Tiff ZOMG ur like so hot. BIFFL lovez ya beb mwah xoxo

Kristy: Totz on herself!!!

Julia: Totz!

Kristy: How's the pics?

Julia: Ba ha ha...rofl. Brb after I vomit! (*They both laugh.*)

Tiffany: Hey Britt...truth box?? (*They both laugh.*)

Brittany: Chyea?!

Tiffany: (*Thinking of something to write.*) Ummmmmm...(Types.) You skanky bf stealer.

Brittany: (*Typing.*) No one likes chu! Backstabber!

Tiffany: Enter! (*They laugh.*)

Julia: Kristy! WTH?? Truthbox...

Kristy: (*Reads the comment Tiffany just sent.*) OH! That is sooo Tiff! COW!

Julia: Comment back?

Kristy: You do it.

Julia: (*Typing.*) Stop commenting my truth box. Brad dumped chu. Get ova it. Enter!

Tiffany: (*Typing back.*) LOL you can have him! Fyi he's dud anyway.

Kristy: (Typing back.) Chyea right!

Julia: Totz jealous of chu.

Kristy: Totz!

Tiffany: (*Typing.*) Btw he's using u to do his assignments!

Kristy: (*Typing.*)That's totz a lie!

Tiffany: (*Typing.*) Nuh ah. He msnd me.

Brittany: Really?

Tiffany: Nuh! Bah ha ha.

Julia: Wth! She is such a cow.

Kristy: (*Typing.*) Brb Brad on phone. Will ask him!

Tiffany: (*Typing.*) G2g. Places to be...

Julia: Chyea right!

Kristy: (*Typing.*) 'fraid u been sprung Tiff!? Lol.

Brittany: Now what?

Tiffany: Block her?

Brittany: Block her! (*Presses keys on the computer.*)

Julia: Ha she's blocked you!

Kristy: Ha ha totz cut!!!

Julia: Totz! (*Pause while she signs out.*) Maccas?

Kristy: Chyea! (*They get up and walk off.*)

Brittany: Ha ha totz cut!!!

Tiffany: Totz! (*Pause while she signs out.*) Maccas?

Brittany: Chyea! (*They get up and walk off.*)

Improvs

This section includes photos to stimulate improvisations and script writing.

IMPROVS

Create your own improvisation including two of the following emotions…

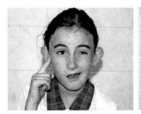  

Confused   Excited   Bored

Grumpy   Intimidating   Nervous

Shocked   Stubborn   Suspicious

Disbelieving   Scared   Tough

IMPROVS

Create your own improvisation using this photo…

They had been warned about the gate…

IMPROVS

Create your own improvisation using this photo…

I loved hearing the story about how Nan and Pop first met…

IMPROVS

Create your own improvisation using this photo...

This was no ordinary book...

IMPROVS

Create your own improvisation using this photo…

The bully

IMPROVS

Create your own improvisation using this photo…

Grandma's locket was very special…

IMPROVS

Create your own improvisation using this photo…

This would be the best surprise yet!!

IMPROVS

Create your own improvisation using this photo…

My big brother teaches me heaps of cool stuff…

IMPROVS

Create your own improvisation using this photo...

No one knew for sure who the occupant of the old shed was.

IMPROVS

Create your own improvisation using this photo…

I'm not saying sorry…

IMPROVS

Create your own improvisation using this photo...

Our old neighbour had so many stories to tell, but the best one was about the scar on his leg...

IMPROVS

Create your own improvisation using this photo…

The letter

IMPROVS

Create your own improvisation using this photo…

They were not alone…

IMPROVS

Create your own improvisation using this photo…

He wished just for once they would laugh at his jokes…

IMPROVS

Create your own improvisation using this photo...

Someone was watching...

IMPROVS

Create your own improvisation using this photo...

Outcast...

IMPROVS

Create your own improvisation using this photo…

Strange things happened whenever we got out
Granddad's camera…

IMPROVS

Create your own improvisation using this photo…

This was turning out to be the worst day ever…

IMPROVS

Create your own improvisation using this photo…

The message in the bottle was two years old…

IMPROVS

Create your own improvisation using this photo…

Secrets…

IMPROVS

Create your own improvisation using this photo…

When they looked back they couldn't see Robert anywhere…

Lightning Source UK Ltd.
Milton Keynes UK
UKOW032346301112

202986UK00006B/353/P